Unlimited Clients!

The Playbook for Consultants, Coaches and Entrepreneurs Who Want High Paying Clients and Speaking Gigs (Influencer Marketing and Branding)

KEVIN KRUSE

www.KevinKruse.com

First Edition

Build A Massive Audience
In An Hour A Day (With $0 On Marketing)

Do you want to **BUILD YOUR PERSONAL BRAND** as a coach, consultant, author, creative artist, small business owner, or entrepreneur?

Based on his own success as an **Inc. 500 entrepreneur** and *New York Times* bestselling author and global speaker, Kevin Kruse reveals how to:

- Become a go-to **Thought Leader** in less than a year

- Quickly build your audience using *other people's* Facebook groups with the **Visiting-Sherpa Strategy**

- Turn newsletter subscribers into "SuperFans" who buy *everything* you release with the **Ben Franklin Effect** (repeat this every week)

- Generate sales from even the smallest email list with the **Intimate Attention Secret**

- Discover your subscribers' true interests and needs with the **Reply-Challenge Technique**

- Learn the secret to making an impact and creating a life that truly matters from the **Gussie Crittle Story**

- **BONUS!** FREE Online Course **"Master Your Personal Brand"** ($197 Value)

GET MY **FREE CHEAT SHEET**

These are the EXACT same steps I use to build and maintain my personal brand, which generates a high six-figure income as a consultant, speaker, and author.

"The 12 Things Ultra Successful Thought Leaders Do Differently To Build Their Personal Brand, Grow Their Tribe, And Make A Difference In The World"

Just Go To The Link Below – GET IT NOW!

www.MasterYourPersonalBrand.com

CONTENTS

Imagine If You Were 'Famous' In Your Niche

Wouldn't it feel great to wake up to emails from people saying you changed their life? Here's one I received recently:

> *Kevin, Four years ago I wrote you a letter thanking you for writing a book that has changed my life! Today I saw the fruit of your mentorship, just this hour my little office beat the financial goal we set.* –Rebecca Day

How would it feel to get emails asking about your speaking fee and availability *every single week*, like the one below?

From: Mike L████████████████████
Subject: Speaking availability and fee

Hello,

I'm with a company called ████████ We produce a leadership conference each year and the theme this year is on engagement. I came across a video of Kevin's and was impressed. We are still finalizing dates but we have November 9th and 10th penciled in . We would looking for a 60-75 minute keynote on one of these days. Would Kevin be available and what is his speaking fee?

Thank you,
Mike L████

Imagine having a backlog of high-value clients who pay you for your *value*, not just for your time. Below is a picture of the $14,000 check I received from a hospital after I worked with their executives for *one hour* (today I make $25,000 per speech).

How would your life change if you could package your wisdom into a book that thousands of people would buy? The Amazon report below shows I made over $7,000 in royalties last month from paperback copies alone (eBook and audio book sales double this figure).

Results

Payment information is available 72 hours after payment is made.

Sales Period	Payment Date	Payment Type		Subtotal	Payment Amount	Payment ID	
Total			-		$7,232.39		
Jun 2016	2016-07-29	Direct Deposit	-	€214.30	$237.42	38949355	Details
Jun 2016	2016-07-29	Direct Deposit	-	£327.25	$430.54	39133156	Details
Jun 2016	2016-07-29	Direct Deposit	-	$6,564.43	$6,564.43	39318712	Details

And finally, while online courses are the smallest part of my business, can you imagine how much fun it is to wake up and discover you gained a new customer and earned enough to cover dinner at a four star restaurant? The automated email below shows that I made $197.00 last night *at 2:48 AM*, while I was fast asleep.

From: **The Kruse Group** <noreply@samcart.com>
Date: Wed, Aug 31, 2016 at 2:48 AM
Subject: You've made a sale! Order #404716
To: ████@kevinkruse.com

Bill To	Order ID: #404716
stephen███████	**Receipt Date**: August 31st, 2016
███████@gmail.com	
07739315104	

Master Your Minutes	$197.00
Total	**$197.00**

You can have this level of impact, too, whether you are a fitness trainer, career coach, internet marketer, consultant, author, speaker, podcaster, creative artist, or any other kind of entrepreneur.

But let me be clear: I do not guarantee that you will achieve what I'm achieving!

Why?

Primarily because most of you will never even finish this book, let alone put its ideas into practice. And who knows, maybe your service or product is bad. Maybe you have a terrible personality. Who knows?

But if you will implement what I show you—it's actually quite easy to do—you will definitely build your brand and grow your audience (i.e., your platform, your tribe, your list) without having to spend any money on social media ads, affiliate programs, cold callers, or any other marketing.

And you'll do it authentically and wholeheartedly, one person at a time, in just an hour a day.

Kevin Kruse
Philadelphia, PA

CHAPTER 1

The Relevance Of Irrelevance

Is it just me or does the world seem like a really lonely place lately? I mean, how often do you feel truly connected with someone? When is the last time you felt truly special?

Ignored By Our Friends And Family

Hopefully, your wife or husband (or BF or GF) makes you feel special. Maybe on your anniversary? But I'll refrain from listing by name all my friends and family members who describe their birthdays as, "Same as usual, I got a card. One year he didn't even sign it!" Or several who've said of their wedding anniversary, "Eh, what's the point? We've been together forever."

Maybe your friends make you feel special on your birthday, although that sure seems to have deteriorated to an endless stream of "Happy Birthday!" messages on your Facebook page. Followed by your obligatory status update the next day, "Thank you everyone for the birthday messages!"

I'm kind of surprised Facebook hasn't just automated both sides of that equation. It could be a new option under Settings, "Would you like us to automatically wish all your friends a happy birthday on their special day so you never forget?" Do you know how many people would check yes to that?

Enough about our families and friends—after all, they're so "crazy busy" these days!

Maybe your neighbors make you feel special?

Oh right, we know from Robert Putnam's research in *Bowling Alone* that over the last hundred years we've become increasingly disconnected from our communities. A 2015 study by City Observatory found that one-third of Americans say they have *never* interacted with their neighbors.

I find that ridiculous. My neighbors to the left are a lovely retired couple named Frank and Joanne (or is it Joan?). And to the right are Kevin, Aubrey, and their three adorable little kids whose names are…. OK, well at least I know the parents' names.

And I certainly interact with my neighbors. Over the last eight years that I've lived here, I once talked to them when my teen daughters were going to throw a party. *If it gets too loud, just text me before you call the police!* And there was that embarrassing time when Kevin came over to tell me that he was worried my dying tree might fall into his yard and crush his children. *Oops.*

Well anyway, enough about family, friends, and neighbors. Let's talk about the people we truly love—celebrities! You know…movie stars, rappers, and athletes.

I'm Warning You With Peace And Love

I'm not even going to spend much time on this one. I mean, except for when celebrities shout, "This is for the fans!" or "I love you too!" during an acceptance speech at an awards ceremony, we don't really expect celebrities to talk to us as individuals or to make us feel uniquely special. I mean, that's part of their celebrity.

In fact, it's their public declarations of *detachment* that stand out most. As I write this, one month ago Justin Bieber put the public on notice through an Instagram post:

> *If you happen to see me out somewhere know that I'm not gonna take a picture I'm done taking pictures.*

And just two weeks later, the TMZ headline screamed, "Justin Bieber Throws Down In A Huge Fist Fight!" Apparently the Biebs lost his cool when a much larger man asked him for an autograph for his daughter.

As a Howard Stern listener, Bieber's public declaration reminded me of the often looped and scoffed at video declaration by former Beatle drummer, Ringo Starr, who proclaimed:

> *This is a serious message... peace and love, peace and love... after the 20th of October do not send fan mail to any address that you have. Nothing will be signed after the twentieth of October. If that's the date on the envelope, it's going to be tossed. I'm warning you with peace and love, but I have too much to do. So no more fan mail. And no objects to be signed. Nothing! Anyway, peace and love, peace and love.*

Just because you declare "peace and love" as you stiff arm your fans doesn't mean they won't feel disappointed, hurt, or ignored. At this point I think Ringo is more famous for this wacky proclamation than for anything he has done with a drum kit.

And despite the promise of social media, when it comes to celebrities, it's more like a bullhorn than anything truly social. Let me scan the feeds of the current top 10 most followed Twitter celebrities: Katy Perry, Justin Bieber, Taylor Swift, Lady Gaga, Ellen DeGeneres, Justin Timberlake, Kim Kardashian West, Britney Spears, Cristiano Ronaldo, and Selena Gomez.

I'm looking for @replies, meaning the number of times a celebrity has actually sent a message to one person rather than made some kind of mass broadcast announcement.

There are none from any of them for the last month. Well, that's not exactly true. Bieber sent a tweet to Kanye West to congratulate him on landing the Adidas contract, and Ellen sends direct happy birthday tweets to her celebrity friends.

Taking The 'Social' Out Of Social Media

Ahh, the good old days when social media was actually social. Facebook was where you shared with friends (not parents, friends!). Twitter was where you'd DM people instead of sending an SMS, and you could publicly share what you were doing so others would come out and join you.

But big business changed movements like they always do, and new tools made it easy for social media to be used for *mass marketing to mass audiences*.

Marketers now use automation tools like Hubspot and Buffer and Meet Edgar to pump out an endless stream of generic memes, article previews, and calls to action. (By the way, I'm guilty of this, too.)

We've gotten to the point where 6 in 10 people share links without even clicking the link and reading the source article (source: *Washington Post*, "6 in 10 of you will share this link without reading it, a new, depressing study says").

The Facebook newsfeed became so impersonal—so filled with ads and company promotional posts—that the company had to change their algorithm to let the human aspect back in.

Automation tools have even ruined the party at places like Instagram. Called bots, tools like Instagress, Socedo, and Archie can be set on autopilot to do a company's likes, comments, and follows.

Just pick a hashtag of a topic you are promoting and set the robots free. Very quickly you'll have thousands of new followers. And that's great if you just want a mass audience in order to continue your mass marketing ways, but how effective is this at actually engaging your followers? How special do the new followers feel?

Email Newsletters That Just Aren't Read

Despite the title of the Godzilla marketing book of modern times—*Permission Marketing* by Seth Godin—getting permission to add someone to your email list doesn't seem to mean much these days.

People who send email blasts consider a 15—20% open rate to be a really good. *In other words, email blasts fail to reach 80% of your audience—on a good day.* And among the 2 in 10 who do open your newsletter, you're lucky if 1 in 10 actually clicks to read more or to check out whatever you're trying to sell them. Permission marketing is *more* personal than TV, radio, and print ads, but if an email blast falls in the woods and nobody is there to read it...

Ignored As A Customer

Last year, I was researching the productivity habits of successful entrepreneurs for my book, *15 Secrets Successful People Know About Time Management*. So, of course, I reached out to hundreds of successful and busy people.

I started with the successful people who I was a customer of. Surely, they'd be the easiest to get access to. As a marketing junkie, I spend more money than I probably should on online courses, mastermind groups, conferences, and other events. Maybe the business owners of these companies would be a good place to start?

I reached out to Brendan Burchard, who I've given thousands of dollars to, attended his live events, and even reviewed his book on *Forbes* when it was launched. I reached out with some variation of, "I'm a *New York Times* bestselling author, and I'd like to include you in my next book. Could we do a quick interview over the phone or email?"

No response.

I reached out to Jeff Walker, who seems like a down-to-earth guy. Lives in Durango, Colorado, and all that. I've gone through his Product Launch Formula course twice. His very sweet assistant got back to me to let me know he got my message, but he was "really busy."

That was a lot more than I got from Michael Hyatt. I was a paying member of his Platform University. Customer or not, I just got an automated response in reply to my email stating:

> *"Thanks for your email. This message is to let you know that we have received your email. Please note that our customer support hours are Monday through Friday from 8am to 4pm Central Time. One of my team members will be in touch with you in the coming days to assist you with your request."*

That really left me with a warm and fuzzy feeling.

Well, clearly having given someone a lot of money doesn't seem to matter when it comes to getting a personal response.

Ignored Even As A "Journalist"

So I gave up on that whole I've-given-you-a-lot-of-money-so-will-you-reply-to-my-email-angle and just went after all the most notable entrepreneurs I could think of. I unabashedly played my "journalist card" as both a *New York Times* bestselling author and also a *Forbes* contributor.

I reached out to all the stars on the TV show *Shark Tank*. I reached out to Daymond John, Lori Greiner, Kevin O'Leary, and Robert Herjavec multiple times, through multiple channels. No response.

Barbara Corcoran responded with a long email explaining that she was too busy to respond with a short email.

But Mark Cuban—the most successful entrepreneur of them all—*did* respond back with a clever answer in only 61 minutes. *Interesting.* The most successful guy on that show is the only one who responded to a cold email from a stranger.

I sent emails through multiple channels to the CEOs of Apple, Microsoft, Tesla, Amazon, and Google—nothing, nothing, and more nothing. No response.

I would eventually reach out to just over 800 entrepreneurs—asking for productivity advice to include in my book—and I received replies from 239 of them. Depending on how you look at it, the glass is 30% full or 70% empty.

It's worth repeating, however, that I was reaching out as an author and journalist, who didn't just have a question, but was also offering the opportunity for some free publicity.

And 7 out of 10 people didn't respond at all.

That's right, 70% weren't interested in being profiled on *Forbes, HuffPo, Medium,* on my podcast, and in a bestselling book!

What would the response rate have been if I was just a 20-year-old kid emailing them with a positive comment or business question with nothing to offer in return?

They Owe Us Nothing

Do I sound bitter? I'm not. (Maybe disappointed.)

Let me be really clear: I'm not suggesting that all these people who play to the masses but ignore individuals are wrong. I agree with Justin Bieber when he said on his Instagram rant:

"And people who say, 'But I bought ur album,' know that you got my album and you got what you paid for... AN ALBUM! It doesn't say in fine print whenever you see me you also get a photo."

I'm not suggesting that all the people who ignored my personal outreach were wrong to do so. There are really good and logical reasons why successful people *should and do* ignore us. For example:

- They're just too busy to respond to all incoming requests; if you get hundreds or thousands of messages a day, there is just no physical way to respond.
- They're making enough money, selling enough albums, have enough customers, without responding to all the people who contact them; they just don't need "more."
- They already have hundreds/thousands/millions of fans; they don't need to win a new one or worry about keeping them happy.
- They already help plenty of people through charitable donations or providing wisdom in their books and appearances.
- They give personal answers to people who pay for the privilege—like those who join their mastermind group or something like that.

I totally get it. My point isn't that people who ignore us are jerks. They're not. And clearly you don't need to respond to everyone individually in order to be successful.

The "Major Key"

My key point—the "major key" as DJ Khaled would say—is a simple one.

In our hyper-connected noisy world, ironically, we don't get very much personal attention. We may actually feel less connected to other humans than at any other time. We just assume we'll be ignored by our favorite companies, celebrities, politicians, and so on. We don't think anyone will care about what we say, write, or ask. Being ignored is the new normal.

And this reality is your opportunity.

"

Mass marketing to mass audiences doesn't change the world; individual attention does.
#IntimateAttention

Instagram/Snapchat: @KevinAuthor
Twitter: @Kruse

CHAPTER #2

Intimate Attention—The Way To Stand Out, Create Fans, And Change The World

You are David and your competitors are all Goliaths. How can you compete when you don't have their money, their fame, their track record?

Are you ready for the ultimate secret?

"OMG! I'm so excited…"

"Oh my gosh, I got picked as Monkey of the Month!" My daughter, Amanda, 16-years-old at the time, just got this special honor from rising pop star, Max Schneider.

Justin Bieber fans are called Beliebers. Lady Gaga fans are called Little Monsters. And Max Schneider for some odd reason—I'm sure my daughter would tell me, but I'm not asking—calls his fans Schneider Monkeys.

Apparently, each month Schneider picks one person who has been especially active promoting his stuff on Twitter and acknowledges their efforts by naming them "Monkey of the Month."

(By the way, I'm suddenly feeling very inadequate that my fans don't have some kind of cool nickname. So if the three of you out there want to huddle up and pick a name, maybe... Kruse Nation? The KayKay's? Krustaceans?)

More recently, my daughter, Natalie, was surprised and excited when a professional photographer, Marco Secchi, followed her back on Twitter and even retweeted her tweet.

And my son, Owen, now 13-years-old, records himself playing video games and uploads them to YouTube. He gets very excited every time a big "YouTuber" (i.e., YouTube video star) likes or comments on one of his videos.

My teenagers—*all* teens—get very excited when they get some kind of attention from a "celebrity". It doesn't take much. A simple "like" on a tweet. A simple "cool video" comment on YouTube. A simple name check when doing a Q&A session.

And what does this have to do with growing your business?

Everything.

Gary Vaynerchuk's Superpower

While conducting research for this book, I stumbled upon a great article by author, speaker, and founder of *Convince & Convert*, Jay Baer (jaybaer.com). In "11 Things Donald Trump Stole From the Gary Vaynerchuk Playbook," he wrote:

> *Gary (and Donald Trump) share a superpower in their ability to make people feel like they are having a private conversation with them, even in a crowded room.*

This is the gift of intimacy through attention, and it's a rare one.

I was struck by that phrase:

the gift of intimacy through attention.

That's the phrase that describes the power of one-to-one authentic connection; of saying thank you to one person at a time; to answering every question you get asked.

While Baer used that phrase to describe how Vaynerchuk connects so personally in a live setting, I think it's just as true of how "GaryVee" connects with so many of his fans on a daily basis.

I'm not talking about how Vaynerchuk or others "authentically" reach their masses of fans through raw video clips of their daily lives and stream of conscious thoughts.

I'm talking about how Vaynerchuk has spent thousands of hours tweeting back to one person at a time, and how he'll solicit questions on Snapchat and record video answers to each individual follower.

Intimacy through attention.

Brady Anderson #Fail

I have two baseball stories for you, about two very different ball players and the impact they had on their fans.

Dave Chesson is a successful author and entrepreneur who spends an inordinate amount of time interacting with fans on a one-to-one basis. He responds to emails, answers questions in online forums, and is way more responsive than he has to be. So I asked Chesson, why? Why does he do it?

When I was a kid, I happened to run into my favorite baseball player, Brady Anderson. There he was, at a non-baseball event eating a hot dog by himself. Being a big fan, I knew who he was, but no one around him did. I went up and very quietly asked him if I could get a picture with him. He politely said no and walked off. That was it.

Brady Anderson did nothing wrong. It was well within his rights to say no and keep doing what he was doing. But if he had said yes, that would have meant the world to me. I'd have his picture on my wall even today re- minding me of that one very amazing moment. Even more so, can you imagine how impactful it would have been if he had taken a second and given me advice or encouragement? If he had done any of that, I not only would have become a bigger fan, I would have proba- bly forked over the money and bought a Brady Anderson Jersey as well as any other Brady stuff.

But alas, that was not the case. Instead, to me, he was relegated to the role of just another great baseball player that did his time and left the league.

As a writer, I like to remind myself how important it is to give guidance when needed. Those extra moments where you take the time to give someone your attention can be a difference maker... not just to them, but about your continued relationship as writer/reader.

Ricky Henderson And The Value Of A Wink

So we just heard how a baseball player's refusal to give one young fan some attention led to a grown man's desire to interact and help all he can. Now let's turn back to Gary Vaynerchuk for our second baseball story.

While writer Jay Baer coined Vaynerchuk's approach "the gift of intimate attention," Vaynerchuk himself calls it something totally different: The Rickey Henderson Effect.

In a 2014 post on LinkedIn, Vaynerchuk tells the story of what happened when he was 10 years old, attending a Yankees game:

> *Rickey Henderson catches a fly ball to end the inning, and as he runs into the dugout, he looks up, he looks me directly in the face, and **he winks**.*
>
> *And that's it.*
>
> *That wink took Rickey, oh, I dunno [sic], a hundredth of a second of effort, but over the next five years of my life, my mom bought me a Rickey Henderson Jersey, my mom bought me tons of Rickey Henderson baseball cards, and the name Rickey Henderson came up hundreds of times. I forced my other friends to become Rickey Henderson fans, thus they bought Rickey Henderson jerseys, they went to the baseball card convention where he was giving autographs, and they paid their $50 to get a signed ball. Rickey got a piece of all that action, guys.*

While our first baseball story was a negative example, Vaynerchuk's story is a positive example of how a little personal attention made him feel special and also turned him into a SuperFan.

Intimate?

Originally, I was going to title this book *Intimate Attention.*

But there is something loaded about that "intimate" word, isn't there?

First of all, the book would get categorized incorrectly in bookstores. To find it you'd have to search the Romance section instead of the Marketing section.

And I can only imagine the eye roll from my girlfriend if I told her I was writing a book about intimacy. ("Pffft! It's a really short book I assume?")

And it does kind of sound creepy. "Oh yeah, the secret to my success is that I get *intimate* with all my fans." Not good.

And don't even *try* to do a Google image search on the word intimate unless you want a bunch of NSFW images on your screen.

But intimate *is* the right word. While it has connotations related to sex and romantic love, it just means (according to *Merriam-Webster*) personal or private in nature.

And that's dead on accurate.

The gift of Intimate Attention: responding to someone in a personal, private, authentic way.

Rickey Henderson didn't just doff his cap to all the fans down the first base line; he gave a personal, private wink to one young fan.

Beating Goliath

In the first chapter, we reviewed how we just don't expect to get any attention from the brands, celebrities, or experts who we love. I routinely get emails from readers who start by saying things like:

- "Hello Kevin, or should I say Kevin's team."
- "I know you aren't personally reading this, but I thought I'd write to you anyway."
- "I never respond to people or companies who ask me to write them, and I'm sure I'm wasting my time, but I thought I'd give it a chance."
- "Kevin is it really you reading my email, or I assume it's some VA in India who is going to give me a canned response?"

These are among my favorite messages to respond to, usually with something like, "Yep, it's really me. Sometimes I *wish* I had a team pretending to be me, but I like making personal connections." You can imagine the positive reactions I get back in return. Here's an email I received last week.

K▆▆▆▆▆▆▆   Sep 13 (9 days ago)

to me ⌄

Oh my goodness!!

Mr. Kruse wrote back to me!
Thank you very much for your time. You are very kind.

Yes! To start online store is my goal which I have been procrastinating for a long time. I know I want to do it and I know it is good for my business but I needed a little push to really start. Then, I found your podcast. Now it is my MIT for my store.

Sincerely,
K▆▆▆▆▆▆

The "Major Key"

So going back to where we started...how do you beat your competition? How do you compete against the Goliaths?

While Goliaths are sending email blasts to thousands of subscribers on their list, you will send one email to a real person.

While Goliaths are busy updating their social media pages with memes, you will answer a question for one person in an online group.

While Goliaths are using social channels as a bullhorn, you will use it to start a real conversation.

Simply put, the secret is to connect *personally* with one person at a time.

"

Who did you help today?

#IntimateAttention

Instagram/Snapchat: @KevinAuthor
Twitter: @Kruse

CHAPTER #3

But Can You Scale Intimate Attention?

How can you grow a BIG business by connecting with one person at a time? How can you turn your side gig into a six-figure job if you're only marketing it through personal attention?

I know so many entrepreneurs who did everything they could to get 100,000 followers on Twitter. Others told me they spent thousands of dollars to get thousands of likes on their Facebook page. Admittedly, one of my own metrics is "total number of email newsletter subscribers."

Whether we're authors, sculptors, coaches, or consultants, we can relate to young musicians who dream of playing to sold out arenas or reaching millions with an appearance on *The Late Show*. Our success, and perhaps our self-worth, are tied to those big numbers.

But perhaps that focus is all wrong.

The Math of 1,000 True Fans

Kevin Kelly, the notable author and founding editor of *Wired* magazine, wrote a single blog post that gave hope to countless creatives around the world. Called "1,000 True Fans" (http://kk.org/thetechnium/1000-true-fans/), Kelly argued artists of any kind only need 1,000 true fans in order to make a living. He defined a "true fan" as someone who will spend $100 a year on your work.

Whether you consider yourself an artist, a creative, or an entrepreneur, I think his argument is the same. If you're a solopreneur of any type, 1,000 fans who give you $100 means you'll make $100,000 a year. That six-figure mark seems to be the Holy Grail for a lot of entrepreneurs.

I've actually never been a supporter myself of the 1,000 true fans argument. Kelly himself points out that this model works well for solo artists, but what happens if you have three people in your band, or three people in your interactive design firm? Well, you'd need 3,000 true fans to get to the same income level.

My issue with the math is that it's actually really hard to get people to give you $100 a year. That's a lot of money! If you're an author, you might put out a couple books a year that only sell for $5 to $20 each. If you're an app developer, you might charge $3 or $9 for an unlocked version of your app, and 1,000 buyers doesn't get you to where you need to be.

So why I am I sharing the "1,000 True Fans" idea?

Because the overarching idea is spot on. There are two main points.

Creatives and solopreneurs:

1) Don't need mega stardom to be successful.

2) Should spend time nurturing "true fans" and less time worrying about getting to a million followers on the latest hot social media platform.

The 5,000 Fan Theory

Indeed, musician and author Brian Austin Whitney had a very similar idea independent of the Kevin Kelly article called the "5,000 Fan Theory". His more realistic idea is that 5,000 fans paying $20 per year equals $100,000.

You can do your own math by taking the amount of money you want to make each year and divide it by the average price of the thing you sell. For example:

- Dani makes $45,000 a year with her "day job" and dreams of becoming a full-time singer-songwriter. If she sells her albums for $20 each, she would need 2,250 true fans—and to release one new album a year—in order to replace her current income (45,000 / $20 = 2,250).

- Steve works for BigCo making $80,000 a year as a marketing manager. He dreams of being his own boss one day. If he created an online course that sold for $1,000, he would need just 80 true fans.

- When I launched one of my early consulting companies when I was still in my twenties, I dreamed of earning a million dollars a year. I assumed I would need 10 corporate clients that would pay $100,000 a year for my services. Later, when we were making $10 million a year, we had approximately 10 clients, each doing $1 million a year in business.

The big idea is that conventional wisdom is wrong. We shouldn't focus on mass exposure to try to gain a massive audience. Instead, as Whitney says, we should be "Giving the highest personalized service to your small but passionate customer. That's the key."

The Dream 100

I'm routinely asked for advice from new entrepreneurs or want-to-be-entrepreneurs. I always say the first question is "Who do you want to serve?"

Inevitably, I get an answer that is way too broad. Recently, I've heard:

- "I'm targeting business owners."
- "I help anyone who wants to lose weight."
- "Human resources departments."

But the riches are in niches. Remember, Facebook is used daily by more people on the planet than any other piece of software, but Mark Zuckerberg started out by targeting students at Harvard. If you didn't have a Harvard.edu email address, you couldn't use it!

The point isn't that your product or service doesn't fit everybody. Even if it does, you will grow faster by targeting a smaller group.

One of the best business books I've ever read is *The Ultimate Selling Machine* by the late Chet Holmes. In it, he describes his "Dream 100" strategy, which he found to be the fastest, easiest way to double sales every single year. He describes it:

> *Best buyers buy more, buy faster, and buy more often than other buyers. These are your ideal clients. No matter what else you are doing, you should have additional effort to capture them. I call this strategy the Dream 100 effort. It is your program for targeting your 100 (or whatever number is appropriate) dream clients constantly and relentlessly until they buy your product or service.*

The beauty of the Intimate Attention Strategy is that it fosters these dream 100 relationships. If someone has actually taken the time to ask a question or give you a comment, they are signaling that they are highly interested in what you do.

By giving a personal answer, you are establishing an important connection. Almost all buyers need to move through the stages of Know, Like, Trust before they'll buy.

- **Know**: I know this person/company exists
- **Like**: I like them, or their brand makes me feel good
- **Trust**: I trust their claims about their product, I believe them, I trust that their guarantee will be honored

I believe the gift of Intimate Attention is so rare that a single touch point—a single email or video response—can move the recipient through all three stages of know, like, trust.

If I were a personal fitness trainer, instead of putting up a generic website and putting flyers on every bulletin board in town, I would define my Dream 100. Perhaps I would focus on serving only pregnant women who live in my small town of Richboro, PA. Or maybe I would only work with company CEOs, who are generally older, busy, and have demanding travel schedules.

If I were selling my social media marketing services, instead of reaching out to all business owners and marketers, I would focus on the 100 dentists closest to where I live. Or maybe the top 100 restaurants in Philadelphia.

Intimate Attention is the perfect strategy to cultivate a relationship with your Dream 100. Instead of just building up hundreds and then thousands of anonymous email addresses to send out your monthly generic newsletter, you would literally reach out to each of your Dream 100. You would write and personalize every email; you would hand write notes and send through snail mail; you would pass along tips, case studies, and offers to answer their questions free of charge.

Lifetime Value (LTV) & The Value Ladder

One of Gary Vaynerchuk's key business precepts is the value of lifetime value. In a June 15, 2015, Facebook post he wrote, complete with short-hand and typos:

> *"If you make all your life and business decisions on 'Life Time Value' instead of what the value is of the 'deal' that moment you will WIN ... Unless u Die and*

than [sic] you won't know anyway... Soooo... Start mak-
ing LTV your religion ... It works ... Period.”

In episode #103 of *#AskGaryVee*, around the 12 minute mark, Vaynerchuk shares the value of leaving video responses to individual Twitter followers.

The LTV. The thing that I live on. LTV. The thing that I live on. LTV. The thing that I live on. Life. Time. Value. You can watch a show once or twice, or you can watch all 103 of them, which become a gateway drug to eve-rything else that I do for a living.

I think Gary is on to something. When someone emails me with a question—about their career, about their business, about coming back from the brink of burnout—and I take time to give help, I do it without expecting anything in return.

But having said that, I have a feeling that a lot of these same people become not just a buyer of my most recent book, but will be much more likely to buy all of my books in the future.

A multiplier effect kicks in as well because SuperFans are far more likely to buy "upsells". Any well-run business offers a series of products or services with varying price points. In my own case, the "value ladder" looks sort of like this:

- Online articles = Free
- Books = $4.97
- Online course = $197
- Online group coaching = $997
- Public large group seminar = $1,997
- Keynote speech = $25,000

- Workshops = $25,000 - $100,000

I could use mass marketing to a mass audience—say generic tip posts on Instagram or Facebook—and I'd be lucky to sell a book or two. But if I answer someone's question via email, I'm far more likely to get them to buy a book and eventually an online course or seminar ticket as they learn more about me and trust the quality of my solutions.

Scaling A Single Answer: The 4 Scenarios

How can you get the most from a single response? How can answering a single question build your brand with thousands of others?

Sometimes people contact me privately (e.g., via email or Facebook PM) and other times it's public (e.g., leaving me a message on my Facebook page). Sometimes I respond privately only to them, and other times I leave a public response that others can see, too. Let's explore the four types of interactions you can have with your fans:

- Private Question, Private Answer
- Private Question, Public Answer
- Public Question, Public Answer
- Public Question, Private Answer

Scenario 1: Private Question, Private Answer

In this scenario, I receive an email from someone I don't know who asks me a very specific question or maybe they're just saying hi. I take less than 10 seconds to reply back with a very specific answer. If they contacted me via email, I reply on email; if they PM me on Facebook, I just answer with a PM. This is pure 1-to-1 communication.

Or is it?

Aren't the chances good that I've created a new SuperFan who is likely to tell her husband or colleagues at work, "Hey, I sent an email to this guy, and he actually responded with some good advice." My private response generates word-of-mouth exposure. Small in scale, but the most powerful endorsement of all.

Scenario 2: Private Question, Public Answer

In this scenario, I receive an email or direct message from someone asking a question, and I write a response—or even better, I record a video response using my smartphone—and post it or upload it to a *public* network.

Typically, I'll record a Facebook Live video *and then send the link in an email back to the person with the question.* I just say:

> *Hey NAME, thanks for your email. I thought a lot of others might have the same question, so I just posted my video answer over on Facebook. Don't worry, I didn't use your name or reveal anything that is private. Check it out here: [Link].*

If the topic is especially strong, I'll record a selfie-video and upload the file not just to Facebook, but also to YouTube and sometimes even a quickie version on Instagram or Snapchat.

In this scenario, not only am I personally responding to one person, and gaining their word-of-mouth marketing, but

I've just created valuable content for my social media connections on Facebook. In this way, one *personal* response can actually reach thousands of other people.

Scenario 3: Public Question, Public Answer

In this scenario, someone will post a question in a public area. Typically, this will be a question in a public group on Facebook, but it might be on my own Facebook page, on Quora, or somewhere else.

For example, I'm in a Facebook group for authors called "Authority Self-Publishing." I see today people are asking:

- Can you get Amazon reviews before your launch?
- Anybody have experience with Amazon's Kindle Scout program?
- Anyone have recommendations for promoting a book launch using Facebook ads?

Over in the "National Speakers Association" Facebook group, I see dozens of questions including:

- Have any of you created / tried to leverage your own TV show to promote yourself?
- Has anyone here ever done activities or keynotes to address volunteer engagement?
- I'd like to be presenting for more groups in real estate. Any idea what "job title" I might target if I wanted to talk to the marketing person / head honcho at a RE agency?

Whenever I have an answer, or opinion, which is often, I reply publicly in the comments section of that post. But while others leave an off-topic comment or one-sentence answer, I make sure to leave a thorough response, sometimes with links, or even (again) a personal video response that is just uploaded into the comment area.

Not only have I gained one new fan by providing personal help, but I've now gained the attention of the other half dozen or hundred people who were also commenting on that thread.

Heck, I once answered someone's Quora question, "What did you do immediately after selling your company?" I answered with a personal story about how I got divorced and lost half the money. To my surprise, that *one* answer has been read by over 100,000 people and received over 800 upvotes in just two months. How many of those 100,000 people signed up for my newsletter or bought a copy of my book? I don't know, but I'm sure some of them did.

THE VISITING-SHERPA STRATEGY

This simple answer-public-questions-with-value-bombs tactic is the single easiest, cheapest way to get started building your tribe/platform. You are like the Sherpa descending from the mountaintop to give advice to others who want to make the climb. Share your best stuff! What path is easiest? Where are the shortcuts? How have you stumbled? You will inevitably be followed, and many will ask you to be their personal guide.

To get started, just join all the groups related to your topic/niche—on Facebook, on Quora, on LinkedIn, wherever—

and just be helpful (don't sell!) to as many people as possible, every single day. As long as your profile is completely filled out on whatever social media platform you're on, people will seek to learn more about you and will reach out directly to connect.

Scenario 4: Public Question, Private Answer

In this scenario, similar to Scenario 3, I'll sometimes see a public question in an online group and I'll leave a public comment saying to privately contact me for additional information.

For example, once I saw a post from someone asking about templates for strategic business plans. I responded with, "I don't have a template per se, but I do quarterly one-page StratPlans. PM me if you'd like a copy."

Here's a clever response from someone in a group called "FB Marketing Mastery." Someone asked publicly, "Any advice on creating an automated marketing process to generate attendees for a local financial education event?"

To this question, one group member responded with the powerful persuasion tactic of *specificity*:

- "I'm doing one just like this in Cincinnati right now. Let me know if you'd like to chat."

This approach is ideal in situations where you don't mind sharing your resources on a limited basis, but don't want just anyone to find, copy, and distribute your material.

Also, the rules of some groups prohibit links or promotional posts. Usually this "I can help, PM me if you want..." is looked on more favorably.

The "Major Key"

While connecting with individual fans and providing individual attention doesn't scale the same way a SaaS software company scales, the power is definitely greater than 1=1.

At a minimum, creating a SuperFan likely leads to additional word of mouth marketing (the most valuable marketing there is). And when you answer one question in public, you have the ability to reach (and help) thousands of others.

So, Tell Me What *You* Think...

Would the 1,000 True Fans Theory work for you? Why or why not?

(Include #1000Fans in your answer so I'll know which question you are responding to!)

Email: Kevin@KevinKruse.com
Snapchat/IG: @KevinAuthor
Txt: 215-813-1117

"

---

*Give personalized service
to your
passionate customers.*

#IntimateAttention

Instagram/Snapchat: @KevinAuthor
Twitter: @Kruse

CHAPTER #4

Case Studies: Who's Doing It Right?

Who's currently giving the gift of Intimate Attention in effective ways? Who should you watch on social media to learn their ways?

In addition to Gary Vaynerchuk, there are other well-known examples. Dan Pink includes his email address in all his books and takes the time respond to all of his fans. Author and entrepreneur Dave Kerpen will take a phone meeting with anyone, as long as they use his online scheduler to book an appointment.

I interviewed several entrepreneurs, authors, and other creatives in order to get their real world wisdom in their own words (I've lightly edited their responses for space and clarity). In no particular order, here is their advice.

Derek Sivers (Musician & Entrepreneur) Founder, CD Baby

A professional musician and a programmer, Derek Sivers scratched his own itch, as they say, when he created CD Baby in 1998. It became the most popular music site for independent artists with $100 million in sales for 150,000 musicians. Sivers sold CD Baby for $22 million in 2008 and put the proceeds into a charitable trust for music education. Since then, Sivers has pursued many passion projects and he shares his wisdom on entrepreneurship and life at www.sivers.org. He is also the author of *Anything You Want*.

While I had known *of* Derek Sivers for some time, and had been a fan of his TED Talk and book, what struck me was his interview on *The James Altucher Show* (episode 159). At the end of the interview, he gave out his personal email address. Not a web address, not his Twitter handle, not the title of his book—his personal email address. (It's derek@sivers.org by the way.) *Huh, an independently wealthy dude inviting thousands of strangers to just shoot him an email.*

KRUSE: Why do you give out your email address so freely? Why do you still spend time interacting with people on an individual basis?

SIVERS: I want people to email me (instead of just following me on some broadcast platform) because then we can have a real two-way conversation, and I can learn more about that person.

I see it first as just good manners, second as public service since I'm somewhat retired, and third as marketing. If someday I'm launching a new business, I've got more of an audience.

Or if someone says, "Hey, do you know any good public speakers on the east coast that can talk about the subject of employee motivation?" I can say, "Yeah! I know just the guy. Here are his URLs and email." :-)

[KRUSE NOTE: This last sentence is really powerful. Derek actually took the time to look me up before the interview and learn more about my work. He's referencing the fact that I write and speak about leadership and employee engagement. Those who give Intimate Attention best aren't faking it! They actually care about each person and take the time to build a lasting relationship.]

KRUSE: What's your process like? Since you're using your personal email, how do you keep track of these personal connections?

SIVERS: I have a good contact management app that I wrote myself (open sourced at http://gitlab.com/u/sivers) that keeps a database of all past emails and activity from everyone I've interacted with: URLs, location, tags, attributes, interests, for each person. Like anyone using salesforce.com, but I use this for my personal email.

[KRUSE NOTE: At the time this book went to press, Sivers actually announced that he would no longer be answering email questions. He answered 192,000 emails from 78,000 people over an 8 year period. Why? He said he needed to "make room for change." I wonder if he'll return.]

Steve Scott (Indie Author)
Founder, DevelopGoodHabits.com

Steve Scott is an independent author of over 60 books on positive habits and productivity. He has maintained a high six-figure annual income and dominates many of Amazon's best-seller rankings with good writing and by building a massive tribe of fans always eager to buy his next book.

For years, Scott was the most helpful member of various author groups on Facebook, and eventually he launched his own Facebook group ("Authority Self-Publishing"), which quickly grew to over 5,000 members.

KRUSE: Why do you spend so much time interacting with readers on an individual basis?

SCOTT: For some people, engaging with others is a fun distraction from work. Being an introvert, it is a challenge for me. I am not the gregarious, back-slapping guy who immediately warms to strangers. However, I do set aside time for these practices for two reasons. The first is good business. Ultimately writers and bloggers are in the business of relationships. Even though I am not an "outgoing" person, by forcing myself to regularly interact I have made quite a few friendships and contacts that have been important to my growth. The second reason may sound trite, but I do like to interact to help people. I enjoy the feeling that I might have made a difference in someone's life.

KRUSE: How do you manage your time? How do you choose who to respond to?

SCOTT: As much as I love creating processes, building relationships isn't something that can be scaled. It takes a certain amount of time to interact, and every interaction needs to have that personal one-on-one touch. The only "tricks" I use are managing my time and being selective in my responses. By managing my time, I mean that I commit to a certain amount of time every day or every week. I could certainly interact way past my limited amount of time, but at some point, a line must be drawn so I have time to work on business.

What I mean about being "selective" with responses is that I try to answer questions that I think will help many people besides the specific person I am answering in the public forum. For example, in Facebook, one person may answer a question I touched on a week before in another comment. A second person may ask a question in the forums that someone else has given an excellent answer to already. While the third person asks a question that has not been addressed in a while and has not been completely answered. In this case, I would only spend time answering the third because I think it would give the most impact for people who are lurking in the forums trying to gain information by reading other people's problems and answers.

KRUSE: Any other thoughts on one-to-one engagement?

SCOTT: My final thought on engaging with readers/fans is a bit of a selfish one. Your readers/fans are your customers. They buy your books, consume your blog posts, and make you the success you are. It is important that you create content *they* enjoy. Not just what you *think* they want to see/read.

This is where polls and direct questions come into play. I will often poll my audience to decide between ideas for different upcoming books. I will poll them about which cover they think is most effective. I will even poll them asking their struggles with the topic I am writing about so that I *can answer* their personal challenges within the books I am writing. In this way, the reader/fan/customer helps to create the product, hopefully giving them something that is tailored to their wants and needs. When you can answer the wants and needs of your fan-base, you have a book that will be a home-run.

Ray Higdon (MLM Leader)
CEO, The Higdon Group

Ray Higdon's area of expertise is network marketing. He became a top earner as a network marketer himself, and has now built a sizeable company—and presumably also his downline—by teaching others how to succeed with multi-level marketing, too. Most MLM professionals I know never reach further than their friends and family for their leads; others will do generic posts on social media. The reason Higdon caught my attention is that he is offering educational content almost *every single day.*

Content marketing is clearly Higdon's very effective go-to strategy. While most Facebook pages offer an endless stream of motivational quotes, Higdon's page (https://www.facebook.com/rayhigdonpage) is jam packed with educational information like "What If Your Spouse Doesn't Support Your Dreams?" and "How To Deal With Prospects That Don't Show Up For Appointments." And although Higdon has over 200,000 followers, he still invests his time engaging with them on a personal basis, replying to people's questions and comments.

KRUSE: Why do you spend so much time interacting with people on an individual basis?

HIGDON: For two main reasons. First, I enjoy teaching and helping people; it makes me feel productive. Second, it is good business. Leading with value and education is what has attracted our best clients and customers.

KRUSE: How do you "find" the time, and what does your process look like for staying so consistently helpful?

HIGDON: We aim to create at least 1-2 new pieces of educational content each day. In the beginning and during the setting up stage, it used to take a lot more time than it does now. At this point, our content creation can take as little as 30 minutes per day. We do this as we see it as such a high value and return process.

KRUSE: Any advice for introverts or shy people, who aren't comfortable putting themselves in front of the camera?

HIGDON: We have a lot of introverted clients, and I can tell you a video camera is much easier for most than going out and meeting people face to face. You don't have to be perfect and you don't have to try to impress people or be someone you are not, you can simply focus on adding value (education, problem solving) to a target market and attract an audience.

KRUSE: Any final thoughts on the power of one-to-one connection to build your brand & business?

HIGDON: We love using content creation to attract people to us more than going out and getting the business. It is a lot of fun to craft good content that attracts people that actually want to talk to you and connect with you. Once you connect with someone, finding out how you can best help them is a lot of fun, *and* when you do good work they want to tell others about you.

Filip Novak (Marketing Strategist)
Founder, Novakomms

Filip Novak is the founder of Novakomms (http://www.novakomms.com/), a boutique marketing communication agency in London. As I was researching this book, his name kept coming up time and again on the lists of "best marketers" to follow on Snapchat and I quickly found out why; day after day I watched Novak's stories, which ranged from demonstrations of new apps to advice for growing your company and even book recommendations.

When Novak and I spoke over Skype, he explained how he felt that he had missed out on the initial wave of enthusiasm and audience building that took place with live-video platforms Meerkat and Periscope. But in early 2016, when Gary Vaynerchuk announced that Snapchat was going to be the app of the year, Novak was ready and he funneled his own online brand building into that platform.

KRUSE: So why do you spend so much time giving advice freely and answering so many questions from followers?

NOVAK: This is really who I want to be. I always want to help people. I want to be a decent human being and that's really what my personal brand is—that I'm always approachable.

And it's a very good practice for me to define my own voice and to actually have that discipline and habits of being positive and enthusiastic, even if I have one of those bad days and don't want to go on Snapchat or Instagram at all.

KRUSE: Is it all altruistic, or do you see business benefits too?

NOVAK: On Snapchat, I don't have a lot of people— probably around 400—but people who follow me there are *very* targeted. Seventy-five percent are business owners, marketers, go-to directors in large companies. Targeting the right type of people is what matters.

KRUSE: So how do you find the time to give all this Intimate Attention when you're a busy entrepreneur leading a growing agency?

NOVAK: I generally do it in the morning. I'm disciplined with my time. For example, I know I've got two messages on Snapchat right now, but I'm not going to check them because I want it to be on my terms, rather than all these devices controlling me. In terms of whom I talk to and who I choose to speak to, the thing is, it's sort of like when you go to a networking event, you can't judge anybody by their cover. I talk to anyone.

KRUSE: What would you say to entrepreneurs who just don't get it? Those who don't think it's worth spending time marketing in this way?
NOVAK: I would say if people don't know you, they can't buy from you; you can't share your gifts with them. The number one thing that every single business owner needs to do is to get attention for their business. This comes from the marketing AIDA model where you generate Attention, then it drives Interest, then you actually create Desire for your product or service, and then the last A is Action. The number one stage, the first stage, is Attention.

KRUSE: Any advice for people, like me, who are introverts, really self-conscious, and just feel horrible going on camera for a selfie or video?
NOVAK: When you understand something, you're not scared of it, so the confidence rises when the understanding rises. With people that are struggling to do something on Snapchat, for instance, they should actually record themselves first without posting it publicly. When I go on Snapchat now, I don't even think about it because I've done it so many times, but in the beginning, boy, I spent two hours on 10 seconds!

Erica Blair, (Digital Nomad)
Marketing Strategist & Personal Branding Coach

Erica Blair (http://ericalive.com/) is a marketing strategist, a personal branding coach, and a self-described digital nomad. While Blair is well versed in all the social media platforms, it's on Snapchat (@TheEricaBlair) that she really shines. In fact, I watched Blair on Snapchat for several months before reaching out for an interview. What she does better with her stories than almost anyone else is blend educational content with fascinating glimpses of her life as a "tourist" abroad. It's this blend of education and entertainment that makes her Snapchat content so compelling.

I caught up with Blair while she was running her global business from Chiang Mai, Thailand.

KRUSE: How many times do individual people reach out to you online with some kind of question or comment?
BLAIR: Snapchat alone I get like 20 to 50 daily. I have to set aside Snapchat response time as its own separate entity because it's like usually at least an hour a day.

KRUSE: So why do you spend so much time interacting with all of them?
BLAIR: I think it comes down to what I enjoy in life, and that is connecting with other people. For me, that's been a thread that existed way before I ever started a business. I don't see it as a different kind of relationship. I don't see it as a separate category of life, like the people I meet online and the people

that I meet in real life. I treat them the same way. I really believe in the Gary Vaynerchuk model of content marketing—giving value to people upfront without an expectation of return.

I think when you look at how people are making decisions on who they work with, especially in service space work like what I do, it has to do with who do you feel like you know, who do you feel comfortable around, who do you feel like you actually understand who are they as a human being. For me, that's a big reason why I'm so passionate about video because I think video is a really good way to capture who you are as a human being.

KRUSE: So is Snapchat where you focus your efforts? What about the other platforms?

BLAIR: I am through and through the Facebook generation. I was on Facebook in May 2004, which is about three months after it started. For me, Facebook is definitely my social media home base online, and I also like that I find it to be an extremely powerful platform for marketing. I especially love Facebook groups. Facebook and Snapchat are where I'm primarily spending my social media time at the moment, although I do have Twitter and I do have Instagram.

KRUSE: What would you tell people who want to participate on social media, including video, but because they're shy or introverted, they are having a hard time doing it?

BLAIR: I was very scared about putting myself out there publicly for a long time. I literally didn't put my face on Facebook for nearly 10 years. But I realized that I wasn't going to be able to have an impact if I kept quiet and if I kept silent, and I knew that I had something in me to share.

Introverted means that you're often in an observer role. You're really synthesizing, and you have a lot of thoughts and things to get out in the world. You have to realize that your message is so much stronger when it comes attached with a human face and a name and a person that we can see is being very genuine and very honest.

For me it came down to, "Yes, I don't necessarily want to be visible, but I want my message to be visible." In order for people to actually want to absorb it, I need to put my face and attach my name so that it's relatable.

Patrick Mathieson (Venture Capitalist)
Venture Investor, Toba Capital

Patrick Mathieson is a venture investor with Toba Capital in San Francisco, and his platform of choice is the question and answer site called Quora. Mathieson has answered an astounding 1,578 questions. His answers have been viewed 7.7 million times (at the time of this writing), making him one of the most viewed writers in the categories of Venture Capital, Startup Advice, and Startups.

KRUSE: Why do you do it? Why spend so much time answering questions on Quora?
MATHIESON: First, differentiation. I noticed a few years ago that most practitioners in my field were not positioning

themselves as both accessible and candid about the realities of venture investing. The older VCs spend a lot of time pontificating, but it usually comes with a "down from the mountain top carrying the tablets" feel. In other words, "this is the word of God, and I'm not willing to address rebuttal or criticism." The younger VCs generally don't feel like they have a lot of room to be open or write anything interesting, because anything that is less than 100% behind the drum-beat of venture capitalism will likely get them chewed out by a superior at their firm. So I noticed that if I could be honest, accessible, and avoided being haughty, I might have an audience, which means an opportunity to help people and to do a bit of marketing for my firm.

Second is self-education. Answering questions about my field helps me more fully grok the nuances of what venture capital and startup fundraising is all about. Usually when I answer a question (a good question, at least), I don't fully know what I'm going to write until I do a couple of rewrites and a bit of research to make sure I'm speaking with authority. This helps me become a stronger investor.

Third, karma. Personally, I don't believe it's good for the world at large for knowledge to be hoarded, especially by people who are privileged, moneyed, and establishment. I feel a moral duty to help non-VCs understand why VCs do the things that they do, particularly since entrepreneurs tend to be at a power disadvantage when dealing with financiers.

KRUSE: Do you only engage with people on Quora, or are there other places you try to connect with people?

MATHIESON: Quora is where I've invested the most time, but I chat with people on Twitter, Medium, and via my work email address, which I publish online for anybody who wants to write in. Obviously, I'm also available to chat with people that I encounter offline, too.

KRUSE: It would be easy to spend *all* your time answering questions and reaching out to people, so how do you manage your time?

MATHIESON: I'm probably not as rigorous about this as I should be. I respond to all emails, comments, and DMs as long as I feel that the resulting conversation will be productive and helpful. There are a few cues that tip me off to when a conversation will likely not be productive, and I generally don't respond when I sense one of those cues. Some examples are a very, very long initial message, hard to decipher question, adversarial tone, etc.

KRUSE: Have you ever gotten a solid business benefit from your efforts?

MATHIESON: Yes. First, I've invested in companies that reached out to me directly via Quora. Second, I've met people online who have introduced me to other interesting opportunities and people, which have led to investment opportunities. Third, companies that have evaluated taking money from Toba have seen my writing online and factored that—presumably in a positive vector—into their decision to pick us over other VCs. In terms of the dollar impact to Toba, number

three has been several orders of magnitude larger than numbers one and two so far.

Tim Pangburn (Tattoo Artist)
Owner, Art Machine Productions

Tim Pangburn (http://www.timpangburn.com/) got his first
tattoo at age 17, and he immediately knew he wanted to become a tattoo artist. Today, working out of his Philadelphia-
based studio Art Machine Productions, Pangburn is known as
the go-to artist if you want a "cover-up" for your bad tattoo.
It's a reputation that even landed him a feature role on TLC's
show, *America's Worst Tattoos*.

As of now, I'm completely ink-free, but what attracted me
to Pangburn was his devotion to his fans on social media. He
has   23,000   followers   on   his   Facebook   page
(https://www.facebook.com/timpangburnart),   over   55,000
followers on Instagram (@timpangburn), and hundreds of
people watch his daily stories on Snapchat (@timpangburn).

KRUSE: Every day you are spending time giving advice and
interacting with individual fans online. Why do you do it?
PANGBURN: I've been doing social media for over 10 years.
In 2005, I moved from Jersey out to Pittsburgh, where I didn't
know anybody. That was also the dawn of MySpace. I realized I might be able to swing clients off of MySpace. So when
I started, I was just trying to get them in so they would spend
some money.

I've spent a long time figuring out the balance—how personal should I be? But now honesty is the main reason I share so much online. A big part of that is being in recovery. I like to help people. I love when people reach out and say, "Hey man, what you said really resonated with me," or even "You gave me the courage to get sober." And there are people who are fan-boying over my work, and it's very humbling.

KRUSE: How many clients would you say you've picked up from your interactions on social media?

PANGBURN: Definitely more than half my clients come in from social media.

KRUSE: You could spend every hour of the day responding to every single fan who is reaching out to you. How do you decide who to respond to and how much time to put in?

PANGBURN: I'll sit down and tattoo for about an hour, then I'll take a 10- or 15-minute break and then sit down and tattoo for another hour. During those breaks I'll check Instagram direct messages, and I'll try to answer as many as I can, as quickly as possible. I get a lot of comments on Instagram, but I only respond to certain ones that are asking specific questions. I do an early Facebook check and a later in the day Facebook check.

When I was starting out, I would answer every single message, every day. For anybody starting out, that's super important. Answer every question. That's how you build up your clients. But when you're super busy, people will understand that you're busy and might not be able to respond.

KRUSE: What's your advice to introverts and others who just feel so awkward when they're in front of the camera?

PANGBURN: When I was a kid, I would just literally hide behind my mom in every social situation. I was very socially awkward well into adulthood. The first five or six years of my tattooing, I didn't even talk to customers that came in.

It still feels weird recording Instagram stories. Sometimes I'll record something three or four times before I post it. You'll notice that when you watch my videos, you don't see people in the background or cars because I'm not doing it in a public place where people can see me. I still feel that there's an egotistical part, and I don't want to come off this way. And I still hear that voice, *what if people don't like it?*

Now I say, "It's not the external validation that I need, I need to know that what I'm saying could affect someone. But it doesn't *have* to affect someone." If I put a video out that is seen by 5,000 people and one of them says, "thank you" then mission accomplished. And what did it take, 12 seconds of my time? I believe everybody out there has something of value. You just need to put it out there and not care what other people think.

Shawn Thomas (Entrepreneur)
Founder, Ask A Millionaire

Shawn Thomas began his company, Uniguest, as a one-man operation from his home in Memphis. At the age of 45, Thomas sold his company in a multimillion dollar exit. Shifting to angel investing and giving back by helping other young entrepreneurs, Thomas quickly built a massive following on social media under the Ask A Millionaire™ brand. He has almost **700,000 followers on Instagram** alone, and initially answered hundreds of questions on Periscope as his platform of choice. I caught up with Thomas via phone to hear about his practice of Intimate Attention and to learn of his future plans to scale his impact.

KRUSE: There aren't too many multi-millionaires who are willing to spend their time connecting with complete strangers and helping them on an individual basis. Yet, you've literally branded yourself—your company—as an accessible millionaire. Why?

THOMAS: You hit the nail on the head. There aren't many people that will do it. That's why I want to do it. When I started Ask A Millionaire on Instagram, it was purely because I saw all of those millionaire Instagram accounts with the big yachts and the billion dollar lifestyle. All of that stuff, and I'm like, "Who in the hell runs these accounts?" You couldn't find any information about the people, and so I just started digging in. I said, "Wow, if I'm going to do this, I want people to know who's running the account. I'm going to blatantly throw out there that I am a millionaire, and if people want to research me, they'll go prove that I'm a millionaire." I'm really going to provide social proof because there's so many scam artists and people that just want to take money, and I said, "You know what? I've got to be overly transparent in who I am and what my reasoning is for doing this."

KRUSE: You mentioned you started on Instagram, but I see you active on all the major social media platforms. Do you use them in different ways?

THOMAS: Good question. You have to use all of them in different ways because if you try to provide the same message in the same exact way across all platforms, it just won't work.

For instance, Instagram is heavily just people scrolling down their feed, seeing a picture, quick at-a-glance liking it, and then moving on to the next picture. Then you've got the ones that are your better followers, and they'll actually read what you write in the caption to explain what's going on in the picture. Sometimes I write real long captions, and sometimes I write short ones, but they all get similar types of engagement.

With Snapchat, you've got to be willing to basically expose your life because people are quickly judging whether they like you. The first time they follow you and they see your story, they're going to judge you immediately. "Okay, I either like this guy or I don't like this guy." It happens in the first day or two.

Facebook is just the most robust platform that enables you to really have an ongoing conversation in the comments section, do videos and articles, and post up longer things.

I would say my favorite would probably be Snapchat, and the main reason why is you just push a button, hold it, and either take a picture or do a quick video and it's done. It doesn't have to be professionally edited; you don't have to think about copywriting and your text. You just take a picture or a video of yourself and you're done. That's the easiest, and that's the one I probably like the most.

KRUSE: Do you have a certain process or any time saving tricks to reach the most people in the least amount of time?

THOMAS: To create great content across YouTube, Facebook, Pinterest, your blog, Snapchat, Instagram, and Twitter, all seven platforms, there's no tips and tricks. You just have to do it. There are different processes. A lot of people will do what's called "batching" content. They'll spend a week just shooting and creating massive amounts of content, and then they'll hire a virtual assistant to piece it together, and then they'll create ninety-day schedules to release the content in a strategic way. Then you have people like me that are quasi just doing it spontaneously because a lot of my content I do based on what I'm hearing.

KRUSE: What would be your advice to someone who, because they're an introvert or shy or awkward in front of the camera, just doesn't feel comfortable on social media?

THOMAS: I would tell them to not do it. You can't be something different on social media. Your audience will see it. If you're uncomfortable sharing, then you don't want to do what I do. You just can't.

What I would do is collaborate. Write your book, develop your course—you don't have to be the face. You can hire an actor, or collaborate with somebody like me, or just get somebody to interview you.

Peter Adeney (Blogger)
Founder, Mr. Money Mustache

Peter Adeney and his wife announced at the ripe old age of 30 that they were officially retiring. They worked as software engineers for about 10 years, and through extreme frugality and wise investing, they retired not just debt free, but with enough savings to live the rest of their lives modestly, but without having to work.

Now known as "Mr. Money Mustache," Adeney maintains a website and blog of the same name (URL: www.mrmoneymustache.com). And what started out as a simple way for him to teach others how to save more and re-tire young, has turned into an actual movement—and a movement that earns Mr. Money Mustache over $400,000 a year. Everywhere you look, it's easy to see how Adeney has used the gift of Intimate Attention to change lives and to build an online business empire.

On Twitter (@mrmoneymustache), Adeney has over 53,000 followers. When you scan his @replies, you don't just see simple "thanks" but actual conversations. Very detailed responses to followers like, "seems like I'd better look into that story though" and "hmm, good point. Some of our prep definitely looked like work. Even worse, we aren't even get-ting PAID to do this!"

On Facebook (www.facebook.com/mrmoneymustache), Adeney not only posts interesting articles, he leaves long re-sponses to people who leave comments. To one person who asked a one-sentence question, Adeney wrote a three paragraph, 152-word answer. And he begins, "Actually Scott...". Once again, the power of the name check. And Facebook doesn't even compare to his blog, where he has deep back and forth conversations with his fans.

When I reached out to ask Adeney if I could interview him for this book, he answered personally the same day.

KRUSE: Why do you spend so much time interacting on a one-to-one basis with your fans?

ADENEY: The reason I read and answer individual questions is that it helps me know the audience better. I learn more about what they are interested in, and this helps me decide what to research and write about on my blog. Also, many of the readers are experts in certain fields that chime in to teach me more about things I thought I knew enough to write about in the first place.

KRUSE: How do you manage your time? How do you choose who to respond to?

ADENEY: It's a tricky thing since I'm only a one-man operation, and there have been millions of readers stopping by over the years. Even if 0.01% of them took the time to write to me and expected an answer, I would be hopelessly swamped.

So I try to stick to answering questions that seem like they would be useful to multiple people, and answer them in public places (Twitter or the comments section of my website). I spend the time there, instead of answering individual emails, because more people will get to read the conversation.

CHAPTER #5

My Personal Intimate Attention System For Growing SuperFans

How do I get 10, 20, or more questions each day? How do I systematize the process so I can efficiently build my SuperFan list, maximize lifetime value, and help the most people?

Basically, I use email and my email automation software as the backbone of the process. There are four steps:

1. **Invite**: I invite people to ask me anything.
2. **Answer**: I answer them directly.
3. **Tag**: I tag emails of question-askers so I can find these people again later.
4. **Share**: I share the answer I provided publicly on social media channels, assuming it's a question that others might have.

What about Intimate Attention via social media? I'll explore that in the next chapter, but for now, let me break down my email system.

Step 1: Invite People To Ask You Anything

The first step, and most important step, is to invite people to ask you a question. People won't think you're accessible if you don't tell them you are and encourage them to contact you.

I put the invitation in the very first email people receive from me after they've joined my email list.

(NOTE: If you're new to email marketing, the fundamental idea is that you create a "lead magnet" [e.g., newsletter, special report, checklist, or other digital content] that you offer in exchange for someone's email address. You can manage the subscription process, email list, and bulk email messages with an online email management system. Popular email marketing systems include Mailchimp, Constant Contact, and Infusionsoft.)

I subscribe to dozens of email newsletters myself, and the vast majority of the time, the confirmation email (i.e., welcome email) that I get says something like:

Hey... my name is [NAME] and I'm the Co-Founder & CEO of [COMPANY].

I wanted to take a second to say hello and welcome you to the family. Here's what you can expect from us...

We'll publish fresh content each week, so we'll send you an email with a short description of the new article, why we think it's important for you, and a link to read the full article.

We'll also send you emails about new courses, software, and other cool premium resources from time to time, BUT only if it's something that we've used and vetted.... Sound fair?

GOOD! ;)

Here's what you need to do now to get started...

STEP 1: Make sure you're getting our emails!

Whitelist and prioritize all emails from "[URL]" and "[NAME]".

If our emails aren't getting through, you'll miss all the important updates about what's working in digital marketing right now (and you won't receive the full benefit of being a Digital Marketer subscriber).

STEP 2: Let's get social...

Take two seconds and join us on Facebook or Twitter, as these are our primary methods of communication outside of email updates, and again you won't want to miss a thing:

Facebook: https://www.facebook.com/[URL]

Twitter: https://twitter.com/[URL]

Talk soon,

[First and Last Name]
Founder
[Company Name]

It's not a bad email—many companies send no welcome email at all—but it doesn't invite a personal connection. If anything, the focus is on making sure you receive future emails, and if you want to connect you need to follow them on social media.

What *I* do instead is use this very first interaction as an attempt to establish Intimate Attention. My first message reads:

> Hi [NAME], Thanks for subscribing to my newsletter. About once a week I'll send you tips from highly successful people who are optimizing their time and productivity. Will you do three things for me?
>
> Thing #1:
>
> Just click Reply to this email and tell me what you're working on, or what you are challenged by right now. Even if it's small or seems a little outside my area, don't hesitate.
>
> Thing #2:
>
> To make sure my response email doesn't accidentally get sent to your junk folder or spam filter, you should immediately add kevin@kevinkruse.com to your email address book, contacts, or safe senders whitelist.
>
> Thing #3:
>
> If you want to achieve extreme productivity without feeling overworked or overwhelmed, take a minute to read some of my most popular articles:
>
> * Why To-Do Lists Don't Work
> * 14 Secrets To Expanding Time
>
> Cheers,
>
> Kevin

Notice a few things about my welcome email:

1) The tone is informal, like you'd use with a friend.
2) It's personalized further by inserting their first name into the greeting.

3) The very first "thing" I ask them to do is to "Reply" to the email. I'm *not* asking them to fill out a survey, or to contact me through a certain website, or to send a note to my assistant. Being able to respond with a simple click of Reply takes the friction out of the communication. Have you ever noticed how many emails in your inbox literally come from an address like DoNotReply@companyname.com. How rude!

4) I specifically ask, "What are you working on or challenged by?" Some marketers suggest you ask people what they are "struggling with" as a way to uncover true pain points and opportunities for you to solve problems. But when I used that language, I got a lot of emails complaining about their spouses or kids, or comments about their poor health, or other very personal issues. I still get some of those replies, but most of the answers are now related to work in some way, which is the area that I'm trying to forge a connection in.

5) In "Thing #2," you'll see that I actually use my personal email address as the "send from" address for my bulk email blasts. Almost nobody does this. Typically, they come from some strange IT-related name or an impersonal organization name. I just searched my inbox to see where the newsletters I subscribe to are coming from. Here's what I got:

- Comment-reply@wordpress.com
- blog@tomtonguz.com
- reply@mail-1-bizjournals.com

- startupsdaily@startups.com
- shutterfly@e.shutterfly.com
- lunch@publisherslunchdaily.com
- info@davidhorsager.com
- bothsides@upfront.com

THE REPLY-CHALLENGE TECHNIQUE

I can't over-emphasize just how effective this approach is to growing your SuperFan list and to understanding their needs.

The key is that you are inviting them to just "hit Reply" to your email; if you send them to a survey link you won't get as many responses. And by asking what they are "challenged by," they will often reveal their problem or pain points. This can be used to develop products and services that they'd be eager to buy or, at the very least, could inspire you to produce content that solves their problems. Market research and brand building all at the same time!

Step 2: Answer Each Question

It turns out that after getting my automated welcome email, 10% of subscribers actually do hit Reply and send me a message. I read every single email that I get, and generally speaking, these messages fall into one of three categories:

1) general message or thank-you without a question
2) a question that is so specific the answer would only be relevant to the person who asked it
3) a question that is common or would be of interest to many other people

Email Type 1: So how do I handle general emails that don't include an actual question?

Here are some recent emails of this type that I've received:

- *"My biggest challenges are time management and prioritizing. Your book has been a godsend. Thank you, Mark"*
- *"Good afternoon! I am currently working on losing weight and scheduling time for exercise, eating healthy, etc. Regards, Kathy"*
- *"It's week three in a new job and first time in a leadership role. I'm working on a diversity strategy. Kind regards, Jen"*

Although I personalize each reply to these general type messages, I do start with a saved Gmail template (i.e., "canned response") just to save time. My template message is:

Hi [NAME], thanks for taking the time to write and [congratulations/thanks] on [BLANK].

I cover productivity and leadership in my weekly articles, podcast, and books, so hopefully you'll get a lot of value from those. But don't hesitate to ask me if you have any specific questions.

Best of luck,

- Kevin

KEVIN KRUSE
NY Times Bestselling Author

PS - If you'd like to stay in closer touch, check me out on Facebook, Instagram, and Snapchat. I'm @KevinAuthor.

Here are a few important points about this template response:

1) I type their name again to help indicate that this is a personal response. (Yes, an email management system could actually auto-populate this field in an automated reply, but most people don't know that.)

2) I'm not sure why, but many of the emails I get will mention new things in the person's life. They'll tell me they just started a new job, or they recently got a promotion, or they just graduated from school, or just had kids, etc. So I find that often it's appropriate to congratulate them on something they've mentioned.

3) If I don't use the congratulations response, I will personalize the message in some other way. Often I'm thanking them for buying my book, or reading my article, or listening to my podcast, or whatever else they've mentioned in their message.

4) I use the second paragraph to remind them—to invite them again—to ask me any specific question they may have in the future.

5) While I use an informal "-Kevin" to sign off, I include my full name and *"New York Times* Bestselling Author" as an authority reminder. You could use any description or credibility builder that is appropriate in your case. Many generic titles like "speaker" or "author" or "CEO" carry weight, or you could mention any awards you've received or other special honors.

6) The PS line is to give a gentle nudge to the person to connect with me not just via email, but also on my various social media channels.

The goal, once again, with this message is to convey in their mind, "Hey, this very busy and accomplished person actually took the time to read my message and sent me a personal response. Cool."

Email Type 2: How do I answer emails that contain a question that is so specific nobody else would be interested in the answer?

For these types of questions, I generally just reply via email, to the best of my ability, while keeping the answer short. I still use the email template as a starting point, but will add a few sentences as my answer.

Below are recent examples of my short answers. Without the questions, they're out of context, but you can see that I really just type one to three sentences in most cases.

- "I freakin' hate prospecting, too. The only way I ever got to the point where I enjoyed it was when I created some educational materials and then just asked people if they wanted them."
- "You must be in a good school or a challenging honors program to have a senior thesis in an undergraduate program. I did one too a LONG time ago. Just realize your thesis is your Most Important Task for now, so you should dedicate 1-2 hours every single day for it."

- "...the 80/20 rule and knowing your daily MIT will be key to solving that challenge."
- "It's been a long time now, but I had many friends who took the CPA exam and said it was tough. I'm sure it's taking a lot of your time, but you'll feel like you have a whole new life once it's done."

For these responses, the only template I'm using is the same authority sign-off and PS line to try to connect on multiple channels. I always use their name, I often personalize with where I'm at or what else I'm doing, and I state that I'm not actually giving advice, just sharing experiences from my own life.

Finally, I just answer their question briefly (regardless of how long their email was to me, and sometimes they're more than a dozen paragraphs long). I think that most answers or "advice" can be stated fairly briefly, and I think most people are surprised and happy with any response, let alone an actual thoughtful reply.

Email Type 3: How do I answer emails that contain a question that may be relevant to others in my audience?

Here are recent emails I've received that fall into this category:

- *"We are experiencing growing pains – our most pressing problem is that we need to adjust the management culture of our company because as we have more people, we need to have a more formal management style. This is causing friction amongst some of our key peo-*

*ple – not good – it is probably quite normal though—
see Founder Syndrome. Although we are strongly cash
positive, this is not something that money alone can
fix. Any input that might be useful to us?"*

- *"What do you recommend for how to keep track of all
the stuff that needs to get done? So if you have a bunch
of inputs (email, voicemail, inspiration while driving
in the car, etc.) what do you do with all of those things
in the interim before you actually schedule them on
your calendar?"*

- *"Tasks take forever to accomplish. The amount of time
I need to complete a task is often double or triple the
time I give myself. Your message has so many pearls of
insight. You also seem to be an information gatherer
like myself. I would love to know how you get out of
your head and turn your knowledge and ideas into
valuable business streams. Thank you for asking about
my difficulties. I look forward to your reply and your
newsletters."*

For these types of questions, I generally post the answer in
a public place, and then email a direct link to the answer back
to the person who asked the question. When it comes to where
to post the public answer, I usually post it on my Facebook
page, but it can be on your own blog page, or even more than
one location.

More recently, I've started recording video answers. Nothing fancy, just me talking into my smartphone or laptop camera. Then I post the video to as many of my channels as possible (Facebook, YouTube, my own blog).

IMPORTANT!

Unless someone has given you permission to use their name and question publicly, don't. You never know if they'll be embarrassed or concerned about privacy. I usually omit the name ("A reader just emailed me with this question...") and if the question itself has identifying information, I summarize it and leave the details out.

Step 3: Tag the Questioner As A SuperFan

After answering someone's question, I want to make sure I can find them again in the future, so I "tag" them as a Super-Fan.

Now, maybe SuperFan is a bit of an exaggeration, but basically, you'll have two types of people in your email list: those who just signed up to get your free lead magnet (90% of your audience), and those who took the extra time to actually write you a personal message (10% of your audience). I don't actually remember where I got the term "SuperFan," but you can call your top 10% anything you want: VIPs, BestFans, Q&A, or whatever.

If you are just getting started and aren't yet using email management software, here's a poor man's approach to tracking your SuperFans. Just create a label in Gmail or a folder in Outlook Mail. Every time someone emails you with a question, you just drag their email into the label/folder. When you want to find everyone who has ever asked you a question, just click that label/folder, and you'll get them all back.

If you're using Mailchimp, Constant Contact, Infusionsoft, or some other system, you'll just want to create a SuperFan group, tag, or field to keep track of them.

These days, I just BCC the email address of my virtual assistant in my response, and he tags the email as a SuperFan for me in the mail system.

Step 4: Share Public Answers With Entire Tribe

Finally, I notify my entire "tribe" that I've got a new post or video available. For example, if I've uploaded a Q&A video on YouTube and my Facebook page, here's what I do:

- Twitter: Send a tweet that includes a link directly to the Facebook video, and I'll use hashtags that relate to the topic.
- Instagram: I'll record a video—only a few seconds long—announcing the new Q&A video and direct people either generally to my Facebook page or I'll say to click the link in my bio. I'll use this video as both a normal post to my IG grid and as an IG Story.
- Snapchat: I'll record a video—only a few seconds long—announcing the new Q&A video and direct people either generally to my Facebook page or I'll type out a bit.ly URL.
- Email newsletter: Each week I send an email blast to my subscribers that contains the links to any new content I've posted.

This is another part of the magic of the Intimate Attention System. While most entrepreneurs, creatives, and bloggers struggle to come up with new content, when you solicit questions from your audience, you automatically have new material every single week.

Engaging With Your SuperFans

Day-by-day, week-by-week, you'll be building your SuperFan Army. I've only used the Intimate Attention System for about three years now, and I have over 4,000 people on my SuperFan list from all around the world.

But what do you do with these SuperFans?

First, realize that these contacts should still be part of your normal list. You should be emailing your entire list on a regular basis (my newsletter is weekly), which is the primary way you'll keep everybody engaged. You'll, of course, also be doing your normal social media activity, which your Super-Fans should be consuming.

But *occasionally* I'll send an email blast *only* to my SuperFan list. Sometimes I've got something special for them, and other times I'm asking something of them.

For example, I recently purchased 50 copies of Seth Godin's new book *What To Do When It's Your Turn* to both support Seth and to reward some of my followers. Rather than announce a giveaway to my entire list, I only notified my SuperFans so they could get the extra award. Other gifts I've offered my SuperFans include:

- Discount codes I've received to spread the word about some online event or product.
- Free Audible book download codes.
- Invitation-only access to a live webinar where I either present content, answer questions, or both.
- Free digital copies of my own books.

When it comes to asking favors from my SuperFans, it's usually also tied to a reward. For example:

- Join the launch team for my new book (and get a free copy of the book and access to my private Facebook mastermind group).
- Leave a review on iTunes for my Extreme Productivity Podcast show (and I'll send you a t-shirt).
- Take a picture of yourself with my book and post to social media (and I'll do a drawing for $100 gift cards).

Know, Like, Trust

A truism often spouted by internet marketing gurus is that people don't buy from you until they know, like, and trust you. While it's a simple model—which completely omits things like value perception and psychological persuasion—there is a lot of truth in it.

- Know—nobody can buy from you if they don't know you even exist.
- Like—it's rare for someone to give money to someone they don't like; and it's not uncommon to

give money you don't have to give (like a tip) to someone just because you like them.

- Trust—the ultimate foundation step, you won't give your money to someone who you think is going to steal it in some way.

Your SuperFans are the ones—because you've given them the gift of Intimate Attention—that know you, like you, and trust you the most.

Why I Prefer Email Over Social Media

This chapter has described my *email* system for driving Intimate Attention. Why don't I use social media as the primary method?

Partly, it's the limitation of the platforms. I generally check Twitter, Instagram, Snapchat, and even LinkedIn on my smartphone. I don't want my answers limited to 140 characters, or shortened and filled with typos because of my horribly slow thumb typing.

But even more important, it's much harder to track who has asked you a question on the various platforms. In other words, how do you label them as a SuperFan so you can reach out to them with a special offer or when you're in need of a favor? There are ways to do it, but it wouldn't be easy.

Instead, I use email as the primary way I seek questions and provide answers, and I use social media messages as a way to distribute my answers.

Having said that, I still *do* answer tweets to me on Twitter, and PMs on Facebook, and mail on LinkedIn, etc.—I don't want to leave anyone hanging—but I don't encourage or seek out that interaction. But if you're curious to learn how Intimate Attention works on various social media platforms, the answer is in the next chapter.

The "Major Key"

It's important that you develop your own "system" of Intimate Attention to make sure it's actually done, and in the least amount of time possible.

The key is to let your tribe know you are there for them. Whether you do it in an automated welcome email (as I do) or by posting "How can I help you today?" on social media, you want to train your fan base to engage with you.

Then answer authentically and make sure to track that SuperFan in some way so you can maintain the connection. Finally, when appropriate, share your answer with your wider audience as part of your ongoing content marketing strategy.

"

Be more approachable; not less weird.

#IntimateAttention

Instagram/Snapchat: @KevinAuthor
Twitter: @Kruse

CHAPTER #6

Using Social Media For Intimate Attention

What's the best way to deploy an Intimate Attention Strategy on social media?

Remember, just sharing your life on social media is not a form of Intimate Attention. Posting about your new product, album, book, or house for sale isn't connecting you on a personal level. You need to put the *social* back in social media.

Which Social Media Platforms Should You Focus On?

It's really tough to keep up with all the different social media platforms. *Snapchat? Really? We needed another place to monitor and build our brand?*

One way to evaluate the best social media channels for you to focus on is to look at where the audience is. Here is the global audience size by platform:

- Facebook has 1.1 billion daily users (source: Facebook, July 27, 2016)
- Instagram has 300 million daily users (source: Instagram, June 21, 2016)

- Snapchat has 150 million daily users (source: Bloomberg, June 2, 2016)
- Twitter has 140 million daily users (source: Bloomberg, June 2, 2016)
- LinkedIn has 106 million active *monthly* users (source: LinkedIn, April 28, 2016)
- Pinterest has 100 million active *monthly* users (source: *New York Times*, September 17, 2015)
- Quora has 100 million active *monthly* users (source: Alexa, 2015)

For most entrepreneurs and creatives, if you were only going to focus on one platform, Facebook would be it just because of its global reach.

But a more nuanced and effective way to look at it is to pick the social media platform(s) based on *who you are trying to reach.* Here is my quick estimation of which platforms you should engage your fans on based on your audience:

- If you have a B2B audience, use LinkedIn, especially their groups. You can also find many Facebook groups that aggregate business professionals, especially small business professionals.
- For a teen to 20-something-year-old audience, Snapchat is the current champion, and quickly gaining ground in all demographics.
- If you are targeting women with some kind of consumer product (fashion, beauty, health, etc.), Pinterest dominates.

- If you are targeting both genders in the 20- to 30-
  something-year-old range, with a consumer product,
  Instagram is your platform of choice. (And with their
  release of Instagram Stories, I believe Instagram will
  continue to gain popularity with all demographic
  groups.)
- Twitter? I'm sure it's good for some groups, but it
  seems like Twitter's growth is over, and rather than
  having many 1-on-1 connections like in the early days,
  most Tweets (my own included) are automated click
  bait.

The good news is there really aren't any fatal mistakes on
social media as long as you are available to your fans *somewhere*.

I once had Seth Godin on stage at one of my events, and I
asked him why he wasn't on Twitter (back in 2009 when
Twitter was hot). He basically said he wasn't against Twitter,
but his "thing" was his daily blog post and writing books. The
more time he spent on Twitter or anything else, the less time
he had for his main thing. The audience was aghast. Yet here
we are in 2016 with Twitter dying on the vine and most of us
hoping it goes away.

Facebook and Intimate Attention

There are several ways you can engage directly with people
on Facebook, including setting up a Facebook Page, setting up
and administering a Facebook group, or (the easiest way) just
be engaging on *other people's* groups.

You should have no problem finding a group related to your business or interest—there are over *620 million* groups on Facebook! For example, as an author, I'm a member of the "Pat's First Kindle Book" Group, which has over 15,000 members.

One Intimate Attention Strategy is to proactively create a new post that just offers valuable information. For example, indie author Derek Murphy (www.creativindie.com) wrote a long detailed post on Facebook that included a link back to his blog. He wrote:

> *I went ahead and made a big list of all the things I'm using my VA for and other things I should be using a VA for. If you're looking to work with an assistant to sell more books, here's a roadmap you can use.*

Murphy then included a long list of items followed by:

> *The rest is on my blog. (Nothing to buy there, even my course is closed.) I'm going to add some more re-sources on that page, so if you're a VA and you can do all of those things, and have a page I can check out, comment below and I might add you. http://www.creativindie.com/how-to-grow-blog-traffic-quick.../*

In addition to initiating a post, you can also just be super helpful every single day and organically your name will become known among group members and they will automatically connect with you on Facebook. And, very important, they'll stampede in your direction when *you* eventually ask for a favor.

Indie author Michal Stawicki is a good example of someone who leaves a lot of "value bombs" as comments in response to questions in public groups. Here's an example:

> *In the beginning stages you don't make a living from your writing. In the mastery stage you don't make a living from your writing. In the expert stage you do. Writing is a very competitive and relatively low paying job. I started writing on trains doing my commute to/from work. I still do a bulk of my writing that way. If you need an online accountability coach, contact me.*

Notice that Stawicki just ended with "contact me," which is a very non-salesy call to action, and again, in the spirit of helping.

I'm a member in several different marketing groups and every day there are group members posting questions like:

- I can't get my Facebook ads to convert, can anyone take a look and give me some ideas?
- I'm only getting 25% of my webinar registrants to show up for the live webinar. That seems low. What show-up rates is everyone else getting?
- I'm targeting dentists, does anyone have any advice?

What you see in the comments below each question are many helpful answers. Some are from people who have no possible way to benefit from their altruism, but many of the helpful comments happen to be from Facebook ad consultants, webinar designers, and other marketing experts. If Jane Doe solves my Facebook ad problem freely through a comment, I'll certainly connect with her, and possibly hire her, for more consulting in the future.

LinkedIn and Intimate Attention

It used to be that LinkedIn groups had a lot of comment action and member engagement, but they changed the user experience for the worse and drove everyone away. Currently, the best way to deliver Intimate Attention on LinkedIn is to simply use messages, which is their version of email.

The most organic and natural way to engage with people is when *they* invite you to connect. There is really no downside to accepting invitations from anyone who wants to connect (unless it's clearly spam of some type); I currently have almost 15,000 direct connections on the platform.

Once a day I go into LinkedIn "Pending Connections" and "Accept" all the invitations to connect. I, personally, take it no further, but ideally would send each new person a welcome message similar to the welcome message I send to email subscribers.

While I don't initiate a message to new connections, I do reply to all messages I receive on the LinkedIn platform each day. Today I was asked for my ideas on how to prevent plagiarism of online articles, someone else wanted to know how they could find more clients for their coaching business, and another asked what notebook I recommend. I answered all those directly on the LinkedIn platform itself, but I try to remind people to sign-up for my email newsletter, too.

Snapchat, Instagram, and Intimate Attention

In August of 2016, Instagram launched "Instagram Stories," which is a direct copy of "Snapchat Live Stories." The two platforms are so close at this time that many entrepreneurs are basically posting the very same content to both.

How can you offer Intimate Attention with Snap/IG Stories? It's not easy, but the best marketers are doing things like asking a question with video and inviting followers to answer. For example:

- Tattoo artist, Tim Pangburn (IG: timpangburn), once asked his followers to just tell him what topics he should spend more time talking about.

- Internet marketer, Tai Lopez (Snapchat: Tailopez1), once asked which book he should start writing, and he often asks which shirt or pair of shoes he should wear out for his night of partying; viewers vote by taking a screen capture of their favorite one.

- Many just ask, "What questions do you have for me?" And then they record and post video answers.

On Snapchat, you *can* send video snaps to specific followers, but this is generally viewed as spam and is not the best way to connect. Inviting all of your followers to ask you questions and then choosing to respond directly or respond publicly is the best approach.

Twitter and Intimate Attention

The challenge when truly engaging your fans on Twitter is, of course, the 140 character limitation. But given that everyone knows that, it is in some ways easier to respond to people on the platform because they aren't expecting a long response.

Leadership coach, author, and speaker, Dov Baron (@TheDovBaron) makes the most of his 140 characters and goes to great length to personalize messages. Among his @replies are:

- "Thank you for sharing a great resource, Coleen!"
- "Agreed Melissa. 'No' is hard to say, but essential!"
- "Couldn't agree more, Leigh! Kindness is key!"
- "That's it John!"
- "Great quote, Terry. I've just defined the mission of a great leader."

Notice that Baron is using each person's name in his reply; this is something I almost always do, too. Most would omit the name thinking it's a waste of characters, takes too much time to write, or it's unnecessary since the person clearly knows you are writing to them. But a person's name is special, and when you do take the time to include it, it shows you are truly being thoughtful in your response.

The "Major Key"

It's not *wrong* to use social media for broadcasting (one-way) your message. But given how few of your followers on any given platform will even see your message (most estimates put it around 1-1.6%), and how few will be emotionally moved by your posts, encouraging and incentivizing personal connections is vital for building your tribe of SuperFans. Ask followers to ask you questions and answer them back in a public way. And ideally, move your fans from your social media outposts to your own email list, so you don't suffer from the whims of the social media overlords.

"

Focus on how to BE social, not how to DO social.
–Jay Baer
#IntimateAttention

Snapchat/Instagram: @KevinAuthor

Twitter: @Kruse

CHAPTER 7

Win SuperFans With The Ben Franklin Effect

Ben Franklin is one of the most famous and influential people in American history. The term "renaissance man" doesn't do justice to the many accomplishments of Franklin as an author, scientist, entrepreneur, political theorist, diplomat, and one of the founding fathers of the United States.

Yet few realize that Franklin was born into a poor family, number 10 out of 17 kids in all. His father could only afford to send him to school for two years; his schooling ended when he was 10 years old.

So how did Franklin quickly climb from the lowest lows to the highest levels of elite society?

Ambition and high intelligence were certainly pre-requisites, but it was Franklin's social skills that truly advanced his station in life. Today we might call it advanced emotional intelligence coupled with a mastery of persuasion techniques. And one of the most powerful of his tactics has come to be known as the Ben Franklin Effect.

The story goes that Franklin once turned a political enemy into an avid supporter simply by asking for a favor. Books and libraries were a big deal back in the day, and apparently,

Franklin asked his hater if he could borrow a "scarce and curious" book from the latter's personal collection. Franklin kept the book for a week and returned it with a written thank you note. His rival was so flattered that Franklin had sought him out, and that someone like Franklin would be interested in one of his possessions, that he immediately began to support Franklin publicly and they became good friends.

Does it sound unbelievable that asking someone for a favor could win their friendship?

Surprisingly, psychologists who research this phenomenon believe it can. Yes, our attitudes drive our actions. But it turns out our actions also drive our attitudes. One of the things we hold most sacred is our identity, and we express this identity outwardly by what we say, the clothes we wear, the kind of car we drive, the bumper stickers on our car, and—in this modern age—what we post on our social media feeds.

When someone asks us for a favor and we accept, we feel flattered to be asked, we feel good that we are helping, and we now have an external sign of *who we are* (e.g., "one who is a supporter or fan or helper or friend of Jane Doe"). To maintain a consistent persona, to uphold our "identity," we will continue to do things that show we are a supporter/friend in the future.

As Ben Franklin himself wrote in his autobiography, "He that has once done you a kindness will be more ready to do you another, than he whom you yourself have obliged."

So how do you use the Ben Franklin Effect to turn people in your online social networks and email list into SuperFans? Just ask them for advice and favors.

For example, I frequently do this is by asking a question in my email newsletter. Yes, I ask all 50,000 people a simple question. And yes, I read and respond to all who answer. Among the things I've asked of my subscribers are:

- "Hey, I'm taking the kids to Jackson Hole, Wyoming, next week. Can you recommend any good restaurants or things to do?"
- "I'm looking for some good novels to read at the beach. Read any good books lately?"
- "I'd like to take my public speaking skills to the next level. Who has blown you away from the stage?"
- "A reader recently asked me my advice on _____. How do you think I should answer?"
- "My daughter is attending Hofstra in the Fall. Any tips from alumni out there?"

Other things I've asked for include:
- Help me pick a title for my next book.
- Help me pick a cover design for my next book.
- Which topics should I cover in my new seminar?
- Will you read a beta-copy of my book and give me feedback?
- Will you leave an honest book review on Amazon?
- What is your favorite Thanksgiving side dish recipe?

You may be trembling with fear over how many responses you might receive and have to reply to. The thing to remember is that even when you are just saying someone can "just hit Reply" and answer your question, the vast majority of your subscribers won't. First of all, your email blasts probably only get a 20% or less open rate. And then it's likely that only 1-2% of those who do open your email will actually take the time to respond.

So if you have a list of 10,000 subscribers, and 2,000 actually open and read your email, a 1% response rate is only 20-40 people. That's certainly a manageable number to track and respond to.

And if you are thinking that's too *small* a number to make a difference, remember you are building your *list of Super-Fans*. When you ask a question and people answer it, they are raising their hand and demonstrating that they are a SuperFan.

Using the above example of "only" 20 people responding to your question, wouldn't you like 20 more reviews on your podcast or book? Wouldn't you like 20 more people to share your news on their social media feed? Wouldn't you like 20 more people to order your product pre-release to capture launch momentum?

The "Major Key"

How many email newsletters do you belong to? A dozen? 50? Over a 100? And how often do those newsletter writers ever ask you your opinion? How often do they ask you for help?

The Ben Franklin Effect refers to the psychological phenomena that it's easier to win friends by *asking* for a favor than by *doing* a favor. In addition to your normal email blasts and social media posts, don't forget to truly engage your audience on a human level. How might *they* help *you*? (And I don't mean by asking them to buy your product or service.)

"

Either write something worth reading or do something worth writing.
–Ben Franklin
#IntimateAttention

Instagram/Snapchat: @KevinAuthor
Twitter: @Kruse

CHAPTER #8

Putting It All Together (An Average Day)

How do you keep up with all the Intimate Attention on a day-to-day basis? How do you keep it from overwhelming you?

I wake up early, and although I have a consistent "hour of power" morning routine, I do brew and drink a quick cup of coffee before I begin it. So...

With coffee in one hand and my smartphone in the other, I start checking all my places...

I check my phone for text messages that came in overnight. I don't usually get many texts, but I immediately reply when I do, usually using voice transcription.

I open Twitter and just read all the @replies. Many I can ignore, but if someone is re-tweeting my tweet, I reply with a thanks, and if anyone has contacted me with a specific comment or question, I write back (usually typing instead of video since I still have pre-shower bedhead).

I open Snapchat and see if anyone has sent me a snap. I don't usually get too many. I respond.

I open Instagram and see if anyone has left me any comments. Also, rare. I respond to any comments.

I open Facebook Page Manager and see how many Likes and comments have come in overnight. I Like any comments on my posts and reply to any questions or comments directed at me.

I open Quora and see if anyone has left a comment on any of my answers. I upvote them or reply.

I open LinkedIn and go to messages. I actually get a lot of action on LinkedIn, but most of the messages are spam or ridiculous requests of me, so I just delete them. Usually there are a handful of messages I respond to, often they only require me to say something like, "Sure, tell me more. But please use my email kevin@kevinkruse.com so I can respond better. Thanks." Basically, I'm moving people from LinkedIn mail to regular email.

Finally, I open my email. Remember, this is where I purposely drive most of the action. It's not unusual for me to have 20 or more new emails from "fans" that have come in overnight. I answer the easy ones right away—the ones that don't actually have a question but are just giving me a thank you or a compliment (actually, it's a nice way to start each day!).

I answer the easy questions right away too—the ones that are just a line or two. Again, I find that dictating responses on the phone is faster than thumb typing. For any email question that is going to require a long answer or a video answer because I want to share it with the world, I just sweep it into my "AMA" email label/folder to deal with later.

This whole morning sequence takes 30 minutes or less. My coffee is done and I'm ready to do a quick workout, gratitude practice, goal review, and meditation.

To maximize my productivity, I generally keep email and social media closed throughout most of the day; I have no beeps, vibrations, or windows popping up every time I get a new message. Instead, I generally repeat my morning routine around lunch and again at the end of the day.

The key practices are to respond immediately to anything quick (most emails I can answer within 10 seconds), and if it's going to take longer, I just sweep the email into the AMA folder. Yes, I do practice "inbox zero," although I call my system 321Zero (see more at http://www.kevinkruse.com/how-millionaires-manage-their-email/).

I then schedule separate times each week to video record answers to all the public questions. I like to batch these to make sure I have a decent shirt on, the lighting is OK, I have a lapel mic on, and then record answers for 10 different questions. I'll post them publicly later—usually no more than one a day unless I'm trying to catch up.

Right now I get around 20 emails a day and another dozen social media messages; it takes me less than an hour a day to respond to everyone.

The "Major Key"

If you just intend to get more social or snap more often, it isn't going to happen. The real key isn't volume, but rather consistency. How will you structure your day, or schedule time on your calendar, so that responding to individual comments and requests becomes part of your ongoing system of making a difference and growing your brand?

"

Sharing is caring.

#IntimateAttention

Snapchat/Instagram: @KevinAuthor
Twitter: @Kruse

CHAPTER #9

What If You *Really* Don't Have The Time

What do you do if you *really* just don't have the time to interact with people on an individual basis?

So, maybe you're a hotshot multimillionaire CEO who is jet-setting around the world, closing deals, and crushing financials, and you just don't have the time. Or maybe you are so famous you are getting a bazillion emails a day and just can't answer them all.

What should you do?

1. **Use snippets of "dead" time.** I often respond to people using my phone while I'm waiting in the doctor's office, standing in a grocery store check-out line, in the car line waiting to pick my kid up from school, and standing next to the coffee pot waiting for the brew to finish. For every one minute in your day you can devote to Intimate Attention, you can respond to four people. Can you find five minutes in your day? If so, you just made 20 people feel special.

2. **Use voice dictation on your phone.** Voice recognition has come a long way and is now very reliable on both Android devices and iPhones. Use minutes of rest or downtime to reply to as many as you can. Just this morning I was on my couch with my cat sleeping on my lap. Even though I should have been up and working, I decided to sit with him for about five minutes. With my smartphone in my hand, using voice dictation, I was able to respond to about 20 people via email.

3. **Respond to whom you can.** There's no law that you need to write back to everybody, or write back at all; it's not an all or nothing game. Just use whatever time you have to respond to as many people as you can.

4. **Save for later.** I try to keep up with emails on a daily basis, but being a busy dude myself, there are plenty of days when I just can't respond to everyone. In these cases, I just drag the emails into one of two folders: Welcomes or AMAs. Then when I do find myself with a chunk of time to catch up—say on a 5-hour flight to the West Coast—I just open the folders and start reading and responding. Sometimes emails will sit in there for months. I still think people would rather get a late response than no response at all.

5. **Copy and paste.** You can use an email template or just copy and paste a short email that you will then paste into each of your replies. You could just send everyone the

same generic reply, but that's pretty lame. Especially if they've asked a specific question and you don't even acknowledge it. I think it's better to use a template that has fill-in-the-blank space.

6. **Combine activities.** When I interviewed social media strategist and coach Erica Blair, she told me that she often responds to people while she goes on her daily walk. "That's why I do so many audio responses," she explained. "I'm literally walking and recording my answers back to people." Do you already spend time on the treadmill each day? Perhaps you can give the gift of attention at the same time.

7. **Read everything.** Even if you can't respond to people, you should at least *read* all the emails from followers. This enables you to get into the mind of your customers, to understand and empathize with them at a deeper level, and to become aware of customer support issues. It will give you new ideas that will fuel your content marketing, your work, or both. (And, I bet if you read all your email, one or two will jump out to you each day that you'll want to respond to.)

8. **Read what you can.** OK, you're such Kingpin you don't have time to read *all* the emails you get from fans. Just read what you can, for the same reasons already stated above. Even President Obama still reads 10-20 letters a day that are sent to the White House. A recent *New York*

Times article described how around 8:00 at night, every night, Obama retreats to his office for a final round of work, including reading letters from citizens. Sometimes he just reads them, sometimes he writes a note on them for staff to follow-up. He can't read all the letters that are sent to him, but he can still keep his finger on the pulse of average Americans.

9. **Use a virtual assistant.** No, I don't mean that you should have someone ghostwrite all your responses—I think that's wrong to trick people into thinking they are interacting with the real you. I mean get an assistant who will manage all of your email and other messages for you. He could put all the simple "thanks" emails into one folder, and the "question" emails in another. He could flag/star the questions that seem most interesting or relevant. I interviewed singer-songwriter Rachael Yamagata while she was on her Tightrope Walker tour, and she told me that she keeps up with all her fan messages partly by having someone put all the things that need a response into one big spreadsheet. That way Rachael can batch the process of replying into one time block each week.

The "Major Key"

We all have the same 1,440 minutes each day. I once guessed at Mark Cuban's email address and sent him a cold email; he responded only 61 minutes later. If a billionaire can respond to a few emails from strangers, the rest of us mere mortals can certainly read what we get and respond to many of them. Multiply your reach—*your impact*—by using technology, scheduling, and assistants.

"

Answer 1 question each day and you will have made an impact on 365 people in just a year!

#IntimateAttention

Instagram/Snapchat: @KevinAuthor
Twitter: @Kruse

CHAPTER 10

Beggars And Crazies And Stalkers, Oh My!

When you actively invite the public to email you with their "challenge" or "struggle" or anything else, you're bound to wake up to some weird sh*t in your email inbox.

Before giving you some sample email copy that you can use to respond to these situations, remember, *you don't have to respond to any of them!* Hitting the delete key without responding doesn't make you a bad person.

Dealing With Requests For Money

Kevin, I've read all your books and I'm a big fan. I'm writing now on behalf of my 10-year-old daughter Nancy, who is a leukemia survivor. She'll be walking next month to raise awareness and money for research for a cure. If you could donate to this cause we would really appreciate it. To make a donation, just click...

I actually used to donate money to all the people who would contact me in this way. I usually tithe my annual income to charity, and if I can support those who support me, why not? But I stopped because it was taking too long to click all the links and fill out the forms and track all the separate receipts for taxes; I also wasn't sure how worthy all the charities were that I was being asked to support. So now I just send a message similar to:

- [Name], thanks for your email and for your involvement with [Charity]. Sounds like a worthy cause. Unfortunately, I'm going to decline your request; I budget my charitable giving at the beginning of each year and distribute the funds to a couple of pre-selected charities that I have a personal connection to. Best of luck with your campaign. -Kevin

Dealing With Requests For Time And Expertise (Free Consulting)

Hey Kevin, I'm writing because your work in the area of Employee Engagement has really been important to us. In fact we relied on it as we built our new engagement software platform. It's totally innovative and going to disrupt the entire employee survey space. We'd like to jump on a call so we can walk you through it and get your feedback. What's your schedule look like for next week?

This type of unwanted email is the one I get most often. *Can we meet for coffee so I can pick your brain? Will you read and give me notes on my novel? Will you invest in my new company? Will you call your clients and recommend me as a speaker?* The requests go on and on.

I do want to help people, and do value the long-term relationship for business reasons, but again I need to protect my time more than anything else. So my response is often:

- Thanks for reaching out. Unfortunately, my current schedule prevents me from doing any live meetings or phone calls. However, I'm happy to help via email if you have a specific question in mind. -Kevin

Dealing With Ping-Pong (An Ongoing Conversation)

JOHN: Kevin, I'm totally overwhelmed at work and at home and feel like I'm going to have a nervous breakdown. I can't focus and my productivity is horrible. What's your #1 piece of advice when it comes to productivity?

KEVIN: Don't use a to-do list, use a calendar. Literally schedule everything you want to do into a specific date, time, and duration. If you really want to do something, schedule it, don't list it.

JOHN: OK, big thanks. Real quick, what kind of calendar should I use?

KEVIN: Something online like Google Calendar or Outlook Calendar works well—you can reschedule things and drag them into different time slots very easily. But any calendar can work, paper or otherwise.

JOHN: But I don't really like calendars in general. Feels too restrictive. What would be your second best tip?

*KEVIN: *sigh**

While I believe answering emails from strangers (i.e., fans, readers, supporters, whatever) is a great way to help others and to build my brand, I don't believe I'm obligated to have a full on conversation (unless I want to). Remember what Jay

Baer said about Gary Vaynerchuk's secret: giving the gift of intimate attention. People should be pleased to get the gift of a tweet back from Gary, or a shout-out on his Snapchat videos, or a response on a Facebook comment. Gary himself was blown away by Ricky Henderson's wink. Nobody should *expect* to have a long conversation with you.

In most cases, when someone responds to my response with another question or wants to debate, I just ignore it. I connected with them once and it's going to have to be enough. Having said that, when someone has responded back to me in an interesting way, or they're an interesting person, or they are a customer who has bought a course or attended one of my events, I *do* continue the conversation.

This has led to speaking gigs worth thousands of dollars; I found a freelance writer in Estonia this way; and I've even gotten free fitness coaching in this manner (thanks Alex Cypriano! Instagram: AlexFitOfficial).

Dealing With Creepers (Harassment)

Hey Kevin, Cindy here, big fan. Been following your work for a long time. Noticed you started wearing new glasses in your recent videos. You look hot! Want to spend the weekend in Miami? Would love to buy you a drink and connect in person. What do you say? Promise you won't regret it!

OK, I just made that up. Nobody says anything like that to me because I'm a dude. And old. Oh, and a little chubby. But a lot of young women who have a public persona tell me they get innuendos from business colleagues, inappropriate comments from creepers, and actual crotch shots from a**holes *all the time.*

I think the best advice for dealing with this is to just block anyone who is overtly over the line, and just ignore the people who are borderline inappropriate (i.e., just don't respond to their email or social media message at all; calling them out on their behavior is probably attention from you that they'd like). Call the police if someone is actually threatening or stalking.

Dealing With Haters

How can you live with yourself spouting phony 'happiness at work' BS. You're just brainwashing the masses so giant corporations can continue to enslave us. You're such a hypocrite. You say if we're unhappy it's our own fault while you sit at home counting your millions and write crap. Do you have a boss? Didn't think so.

I write about leadership and employee engagement, among other things, and the person who sent me the note above clearly isn't happy in her job or happy with my words of wisdom. I've heard many entrepreneurs like Ramit Sethi and Brendan Burchard say they respond to their haters. I think they do it because they think it's fun or funny, but they do claim they've turned some people around or even gotten valuable feedback from these exchanges.

My own approach is generally to ignore the haters (i.e., Don't feed the trolls!) just because I truly value my 1,440 minutes in each day and would rather invest a minute with someone I'm more likely to help. But sometimes I'll send back something like, "I'm sorry you feel that way and that my work hasn't provided any value." It's sort of a secular version of "I'll be praying for you."

Dealing With 'I Have Cancer…'

Unfortunately whilst working (and playing) hard I forget to look after an important factor, my health. Last year I was diagnosed with cancer and quickly progressed through stages 1, 2 and 3, settling at a 3c (where I hope to hold strong). There were a few warnings and many things I should have been doing, but I was too busy…

It's surprising and sad just how often someone mentions their cancer diagnosis as part of their initial email to me. Literally, as I was getting ready to write this section, I took an email break. One of the new messages I received included, "I am a recent cancer survivor (within the last 3 years – had a 22% chance of survival) and am ready to get on with life…. When you were supposed to die, every day is a bonus."

I have no canned message or template for these responses. I usually just write whatever I'd write to a friend and then comment on the rest of their message or answer their question. For example:

- Hi [name], thanks for the email and sorry to hear about your recent health troubles…

- Hi [name], thanks for contacting me with your question and really sorry to hear about your cancer diagnosis. I can only imagine how tough it must be right now for you and your family. Regarding your question...

Dealing With Suicidal Intentions

Kevin, I don't know what to do and have no one else to turn to. My life is in complete turmoil. I feel hopeless. I want to commit suicide. -Zac

Fortunately, I haven't had too many suicidal emails over the years. When I do get them, I think that it could be some kind of scam or prank, but I always assume that they're for real. So I do respond, hoping that any kind of connection is a positive thing, but I in no way offer advice or continue the engagement. Unless you're a trained and licensed profession-al, I think your advice could do harm instead of help. Typically, I respond with something like:

- *Zac, thanks for reaching out and sorry to hear you're feeling so badly. I'm not qualified to give any specific advice. If you feel that you want to harm yourself, you should seek immediate help from a doctor or contact a suicide hotline. Please take care of yourself. -Kevin*

The "Major Key"

When you invite human connection, you need to expect a wide range of human responses. Most of your contact will of course come from grateful, polite, complimentary fans. Just be ready with the right response to the 1% who abuses your accessibility.

"

Haters: People who secretly wish to be you.

#IntimateAttention

Instagram/Snapchat: @KevinAuthor
Twitter: @Kruse

EPILOGUE

Life Is About Making An Impact, Not Making An Income

Taped to the bottom of my computer monitor is the obituary of a complete stranger. It's only four sentences long; the death notice is of a woman named Gussie LaJean Crittle.

Back on June 22 of 2014, I received an email with the subject, "I have no idea how to succeed." It was from a Gussie Critle (yes, only one "t" in her name, even though the death notice has two).

As an author and someone who is active on social media, I get about 20 emails each day from people I don't know. But this message was a little different than what I usually get. It simply read:

I cannot speak. Lost my voice 30 years ago. Don't won't [sic] to throw a pity party but I am stuck.

That's it.

At first I was suspicious. Mixed in with all the legitimate questions or gratitude I get from readers, I also get requests from people asking me to donate to their church, to invest in their startup, and occasionally, some attractive woman half my age wants to know if I'd like to go on a date. (As tempting as that last one is, I just know I'd wake up in an ice bath without a kidney.)

Looking back, I'm not sure why I assumed Gussie Critle was setting me up for a request for money.

Maybe it was the unusual name. *Gussie Critle? Where is this person even from?*

Maybe it was the terseness of the email. Her style is so direct. No hello, no preamble, just:

> *I cannot speak. Lost my voice 30 years ago.*

I think I was also frustrated at how vague the question was. I get that a lot—one line emails like, "Please tell me how to become a *New York Times* bestselling author." *Really? Should I start with how to write? Or how to find a publisher? Or how to launch and market a book, or…?*

And I hope not, but it's just possible that I had other fleeting thoughts. *There is no way this woman will ever buy a book from me. Obviously, she isn't going to hire me for a speaking gig or become a client.*

I hesitated, but hit Reply and typed sort of a test message. I figured Gussie was probably some flake or not even a real person, so before I took the time to answer, I wanted to test her out. I'm embarrassed by this now, but that's how it happened. I wrote back a terse note of my own:

> *Hi Gussie, thanks for your note. I'm just curious, where do you call home? I'm just outside Philadelphia.*

You say you are stuck. When you ask "how to succeed," what do you want to succeed with?

Kevin

To my surprise, only one hour later, Gussie replied.

Sherman, MS is my current home. My whole life was my voice. I have a handicapped daughter, it's been 30 years since my cancer. Bad choices in men, school and life choices I am no baby, but I am still here. I just need a way to generate money for me and my daughter.

Now at this part of the story I wish I could share that I actually gave Gussie some money, or found a way to secretly pay her utility bills each month, or that I drove down to Mississippi and befriended her. But I did none of those things.

With her second email, she sure sounded like a real person, with a real question. "Bad choices in men…" actually made me chuckle. "I am no baby" once again declaring that she isn't feeling sorry for herself.

"But I am still here" is the line that resonates with me in ways I still don't fully understand.

And yet I was *still* suspicious. *Am I getting played for a fool? Am I getting conned by some online scammers who come up with sob stories and hit up people on the internet?*

Thankfully, I did send Gussie an answer, albeit a short one. I replied:

Gussie, my only suggestion is that more people are making money from home than ever before thanks to the internet and computers. You seem to be quite com-

puter savvy...you found me! I don't know what knowledge and skills you have--and of course it's always a good idea to keep developing those--but you might browse around some of these sites where people are making a lot of money from home.

Etsy: Many people sell their arts and crafts through this online store. www.etsy.com

Fiverr: People offer to do all kinds of stuff for five bucks. http://www.fiverr.com/

Elance: People offer skills for a variety things (proofreading, writing, etc.) https://www.elance.com/

Shopify: People sell all kinds of goods by setting up their online store at https://www.shopify.com/.

Ebay: Same idea...you can setup your own page and sell things using an auction model.

It's great if you have some skill like proofreading, or can make a unique product or craft. But I know several people that just resell things online they get from somewhere else. Maybe there are some local Mississippi products, foods, recipes, that you can buy and then resell online for a profit.

I just hope this sparks some creative ideas. I'm sure you can find something you can do from home. I look forward to hearing of your success.

Gussie didn't reply with a thank you. She never asked any follow-up questions. I never heard from her again.

For the next two years, I rarely thought of Gussie at all. When I did remember her, it was triggered by some random email request for money from a stranger. I'd think back and wonder whether Gussie was a real person who wasted my time, or was a fake identity from someone who was setting up a scam.

But earlier this year everything changed. Unexpectedly, I received this email:

> *Hello I hope your [sic] doing fine. My name is Timika Crittle. I don't know if you remember my mother Gussie Crittle writing to you in Fall of 2014. My mother lost her voice due to cancer. She written [sic] to for advice on how she can generate income and provider for her family. I want to thank you for replying to her email and giving her advice. It lifted her spirit and gave her hope again. Sadly my mother never got the chance to try what you subjected [sic]. My mother developed cancer again in 2014 and lost her battle on Sept 29, 2015.*

I read Timika Crittle's email and I cried.

Not entirely sure why I cried. I think I was both sad that I had ever doubted the email from "Gussie Critle" to begin with, and sad that I hadn't actually done more.

And I was sad for Gussie's passing and for her daughter Tamika—I've lost my mother, too. In only two emails I could tell Gussie was a unique spirit. I did some Googling and quickly learned that Gussie's middle name was LaJean; she used to work as a housekeeper, and she was 65 years old when she passed.

Timika's simple message of thanks was a huge gift that reminded me of why I write, give talks, and answer emails from readers.

Like most people, although I wish I was immune, I often desire the external validation that comes from vanity metrics.

How come my post on Facebook didn't get over 100 likes? Will my blog article get over 1,000 views? I hope my book hits the bestseller lists!

But now I ground myself each morning with Gussie La-Jean Crittle's obituary. I read it as my computer boots up. It's my reminder to assume the best of intentions in all I meet, to make the time to answer as many questions as I can, and to remember that giving hope is just as important as giving knowledge.

And while I still want to impact many, I now write each new article and each new book with the goal to help just one person.

Gussie LaJean Crittle, 65, of Sherman, formerly of Holly Springs, died Sept. 27, 2015, at her home. She was formerly employed in housekeeping with Quality Inn and Suites in Tupelo.

Services were held at 11 a.m. on Oct. 3 at Hopewell No. 1 MB Church. Burial was in Bowens Cemetery. Rev. Leroy James officiated. J.F. Brittenum and Son Funeral Home was in charge of arrangements.

FREE ONLINE COURSE:
Master Your Personal Brand

In this FREE 3-video course ($197 value), you'll learn:

- **5 Steps To Create Your Powerful And Profitable Personal Brand**

- **7 Rookie Personal Branding Mistakes To Avoid At All Costs**

- **The Simple Tools I Use To Create, Build, and Monetize My Personal Brand**

To enroll in your free course, go to:

www.MasterYourPersonalBrand.com

Did You Like This Book?

Before you go, I'd like to say THANK YOU for reading my book. **Can I ask a quick favor?**

Will you take two minutes or less to leave an honest review for this book on Amazon (because reviews are the #1 way others decide if they'll buy a book or not)?

Keynote Speech:
The Power of Intimate Attention

Kevin Kruse speaks around the world at executive retreats, sales meetings, and association conferences. Based on his bestselling book *Unlimited Clients!* Kevin shares the surprising ways entrepreneurs—**real estate professionals, solopreneurs, network marketers, creatives, small business owners—and everyone can build a brand, grow a business, and change the world** in just an hour a day.

To invite Kevin to speak at your next event,
email info@kevinkruse.com
Or call 267-756-7089

About Kevin Kruse

In pursuit of the American Dream, Kevin Kruse started his first company when he was just 22 years old. He worked around the clock, living out of his one-room office and showering each day at the YMCA before giving up a year later deeply in debt.

But after discovering the power of Extreme Productivity and Intimate Attention, Kevin went on to build and sell several multimillion dollar companies, winning Inc. 500 and Best Place to Work awards along the way.

Email: kevin@KevinKruse.com (best way to reach me)
Website: www.KevinKruse.com
LinkedIn: www.linkedin.com/in/kevinkruse67
Facebook: www.facebook.com/KruseAuthor
YouTube: KruseAuthor
Instagram: @KevinAuthor
Snapchat: @KevinAuthor
Twitter: @Kruse

Acknowledgements

Hopefully you agree with Pablo Picasso, who said, "Good artists copy, great artists steal." While my practice of Intimate Attention has been a long-time habit, I was inspired by the audacity of Gary Vaynerchuk. And big thanks to Jay Baer for coining the phrase "the gift of intimate attention."

Made in the USA
Monee, IL
21 April 2022

95093146R10075